T0375253

Jewels In Her Crown

Jewels In Her Crown

SUSIE WYATT-CLEMENS

authorHOUSE®

AuthorHouse™
1663 Liberty Drive
Bloomington, IN 47403
www.authorhouse.com
Phone: 1-800-839-8640

© 2012 by Susie Wyatt-Clemens. All rights reserved.

No part of this book may be reproduced, stored in a retrieval system, or transmitted by any means without the written permission of the author.

Published by AuthorHouse   03/19/2012

ISBN: 978-1-4685-2881-7 (sc)
ISBN: 978-1-4685-2908-1 (e)

Library of Congress Control Number: 2011962581

Any people depicted in stock imagery provided by Thinkstock are models, and such images are being used for illustrative purposes only.
Certain stock imagery © Thinkstock.

This book is printed on acid-free paper.

Because of the dynamic nature of the Internet, any web addresses or links contained in this book may have changed since publication and may no longer be valid. The views expressed in this work are solely those of the author and do not necessarily reflect the views of the publisher, and the publisher hereby disclaims any responsibility for them.

Contents

Acknowledgments

To all of those who have encouraged me to put word to paper, and then to print, thank you so much. With your continual love and support, you are all special to me and have left your foot print on my heart.

A few shout outs are very much in order.

To my friend, Linda Linderggard. We walk this path together, thank you so much for being in my life.

To Steven Farnsworth. Without you in my life, the life I have with my special friend and adopted brother, Les, well let's just say, the life I have would not be! Thank you Steven for being my friend.

Susie Wyatt-Clemens

To Richard and Roseann Lasater. Your protection and unconditional love for me has no bounds. Your friendship over the years is precious to my soul. Thank you for always and always being in my life.

To my friend Sharon Blackburn: You truly are a friend who would give your last dollar away to help me. You were there during the crying time, and have never left. Thanks girlfriend for standing by me and with me, even in the ugly stuff!

To my grandfather, Leonard Malby: Without your inheritance, I would never have had the monies to buy our computer, and this book would never had been written.

To my friend here in Beaver Valley, Lois Johnson: Without your help with this computer and how to set up my book, how to save it, how to send it, well, all the little things that didn't come naturally to me, a great big THANK YOU!

And to my Very Special Friend and co-author of Rachel's Eyes, Helen Littrell: Your continual encouragement, your love for me, the laughs and giggles we have had along the way, and the editing of this very personal story, Thank You just doesn't really say enough. So I will say, I love you so much friend. Your friendship is on my heart and in my life . . . . Namaste.

Dedicated to three very special and unique
people in my life

To my daughter:

Thank you sweetheart for choosing me as your mom! For all I
put you through, your soul turned them all into Jewels for your
crown. Wear them with confidence, you have earned them.
How very special you are in my life and always will be.

To Swamii Ty:

You always made me find my own answers to my questions,
but always by my side to make sure that what I found, I landed
softly and safe. Your knowledge and guidance on my spiritual
journey, has molded me into the woman I am today and the
strength to write my story, warts and all!

To my very special brother, and friend, Les Pascoe:

Where do I begin? Ah, there is so much! Thank you for showing
and helping me live outside the box! To have the courage to
be authentic, and walk in truth! To live my daily life in harmony
and most of all, Bro, thank you for the life I live, with all the
trimmings. We have an awesome life! Don't we?

Peace To All

Quotes

Behind every dark cloud, is a silver lining, you just have to look.

My mom, Betty Malby-Wyatt

With each full circle in your life, a jewel is put in your crown, to be placed On your head when you reach heaven.

My grandmother, Agnes Malby

Being a victim, limits you in fear.
Being a survivor gives you the courage and strength to change the world!

My friend, Gayle Nelson

Help in the beginning.

National Aids Hotline

Spokane Aids Network

Thank you so much for being there. You case managed me, pointed me in the direction of help for paying my bills, food banks, paying for prescriptions, councelling. Most of all for your support, for being there. What ever my needs were you would find the answers, even a new and safe place for my daughter and I to live.

Strength for the Journey Retreats

Wow! Thank you for being there. Boy, look how far I have come! Without these retreats, I know, I wouldn't be where I am today. You really did give me the strength to live my life, and this book wasn't written without thinking of you, often. So Please, continue on, You not only changed my life but many, many more you don't even know!

I live here in Payson Az., now, and there is even a Strength for the Journey retreat week here. So, I ask all of you to support the Strength for the Journey retreats, in care of the United Methodist Church. Make donations ear marked for the retreats. Thank you so much.

WABA, women affected by aids. Created by Helen Bonzer.

Wow Helen, it seems like a lifetime ago, oh, that's right, it was! So much thanks for having you in my life and for all you have done for us women.

Blessed are you, my friend.

Book List.

Many books have helped me over the years, and listed are just a small handful. I have learned to think outside the box. I have learned how to search for my passion and live in the now. I have also discovered a path of spirituality that has given me the freedom to forgive and find my joy. They all in some way helped me discover, me. All I had to do was want a change, to change the programing, and start thinking through my choices and decisions. To find my purpose, and maybe, just maybe, to help you find yours too.

The Laws of Spirit
By Dan Millman
Published by H. J. Kramer and New World
Library, 1995
ISBN 0-915811-93-6

The Diamond Light
By Djwhal Khul: Channeled through Violet Starre
Published by Light Technology Publishing
Flagstaff Az. 2000
ISBN 1-891824-25-2

Susie Wyatt-Clemens

Journey of Souls
By Michael Newton, Phd
Published by Llewellyn publications
Woodbury, Mn. 1994
ISBN 10: 1-56718-485-5

Destiny of the Soul
By Michael Newton, Phd
Published by Llewellym Publications
St. Paul Mn. 2004
ISBN 1-56718499-5

And these books below, put it all together for me
Your Souls Plan
By Robert Schwartz
Publoshed by Frog Books and distributed by North
Atlantic Books, 2007 and 2009
ISBN 13: 978-1-58394-272-7 and ISBN 10:
1-58394-272-6

A New Earth, by Eckhart Tolle
Namaste Publishing Book
Published by the Penguin Group
New York, N.Y, 2005
ISBN 978-0-452-28996-3

The Power of Now by Eckhart Tolle
Published by New World library, Novato Ca.
Namaste Publishing Vancover B.C. Canada 2004
ISBN 1-57731-480-8

All of Dr. Wayne Dryer's book and Louise L Hay, Heal your Body.This little book not only opened up the physician within all of us to heal, but the courage to try, this list could go on and on, so thank you all for helping me grow and change, and hopefully this book can help others too.

Chapter 1

It was on the Fourth of July, 1992 when I overheard Joe's mother say to his sisters, "Oh no, Joe has known for years he has AIDS!" I'd just started to walk from the hallway into the kitchen when I realized what she was saying. What! I thought to myself, he's known for years? He knew when I met him? He knew the first time we made love? He knew last September when he was in the hospital, when he told me he'd just found out he was HIV positive? What!! What!!!

Quickly, before his mother or sisters could see me, I turned around in the doorway, ran down the hall, and made it to the bathroom just in time to throw up my life! Everything I had been told was a big fat lie . . . I had to get a grip on myself and get out of here. To a safe place, to home. When I finally left the bathroom, I went back into the kitchen and informed his mother that I must have the flu and was going home. "An, oh by the way, I told her, Joe should stay with you for a few days until I felt better" . . . HE KNEW? HE KNEW? Oh God, he knew, and it wasn't an accident that I have HIV . . . he knew all along . . .

Ten Months Earlier

It was in September of 1992 that Joe went to the hospital with pneumonia. A few days later while still confined to his hospital bed, he'd told me he had just learned that he had HIV. "I'm so sorry Susie, I had no idea. You need to go get checked. I'm so sorry, I love you with all my heart. Are you going to stay with me? I won't blame you if you don't. Please don't leave me."

Oh God! Oh God! OH GOD!!!! Even almost twenty years later, I still recall every single detail as vividly as if it were yesterday. The shock, pain, hurt, anger, embarrassment—all the above! The only adjective that isn't there is—forgiveness. And that wasn't to come for many years.

I remember going to Dr. Ruark (my personal doctor) and telling him what I had just found out, and that I needed "THE TEST". I had just been there in his office a couple of weeks previously to get some medication for the flu that was going around. I'd worked at the hospital in Spokane, Washington, for the past several years and minor flu epidemics were not that uncommon. When he called me into his office a week later to go over the test results, he informed me that they had been "inconclusive" and that I would need to be retested in about three months to be sure of the results. In the meantime he told me I should practice safe sex and described in detail exactly what that meant.

Well, I didn't leave Joe. Why? Because I couldn't just bail on him . . . He loved me, he needed me. Or so I thought. And what if I am positive!!! Who will want me?? . . . I just have to tough it out and see what happens in a few months.

Toward the end of September I had an accident on the job at the hospital. With my Operating Room paper booties on, I had missed the last rung on a ladder, fallen, and then slipped on the floor. When they examined me in the Emergency Room, they told me that I'd ripped the muscles along my spinal cord. Oh boy, did that hurt. I ended up on the hospital labor and industry (L&I) insurance with my income now cut in half. I was in horrible pain and with Joe twenty-four/seven. He'd moved in with me to take care of me . . . and I was very grateful. Boy, did he ever love me!!!

It wasn't until January of 1993 that I went in for my second HIV test. Several days later the doctor's office called, asking me to come in and go over the results. Dr. Ruark was one of those doctors who was just awesome—always with a smile and a hug for his patients. I got to know his 'hospital' side when I worked there and everyone loved him. He was also my mom's doctor, and when she was dying of cancer in the first part of 1992 I saw the obvious hurt and pain in him as well as his concern for all of us. He was truly one amazing human being!

The moment Dr. Ruark came into the exam room I knew immediately what my test result was. I saw the pain in his face and the tears in his eyes, and before anything was said we were both crying . . . . This can't happen to someone like me . . . I-I-I-I'm a nice person! I'm not a prostitute! I'm not a drug addict! I'm not gay! . . . I'm a white, heterosexual, 40-year-old single mother of three with one child still at home . . . . This can't be happening to me! Oh God! What am I going to do"? All the time I was crying buckets of tears into my doctors hug . . . .

Eventually I made it home that day, still not sure exactly how—maybe on the wings of an angel. I told Joe the minute I walked in. Actually he could tell by just looking at me. I cried all over again with Joe, while he was saying over and over again how sorry he was, that he would never leave me—LEAVE ME! Well, of course not! That had never crossed my mind. After all, I didn't leave him when he told me! But he also began telling ME not to tell anyone!!! "Your friends will leave you and your family will not be there for you. Don't tell anyone, ever . . . I'll be here for you, I will never leave you, you can count on me!!!" It was a mantra that he repeated over and over until I became numb to the sound of his voice.

By now, several months later, our relationship had become volatile with the mix of alcohol into it. I didn't leave the relationship, even in the mist of the physical abuse,but why? Why did I think this was okay? I needed his money (because I was still on L and I from my injury at work). I reminded myself, who else will want me? I can't tell anyone what I am really going through . . . . they might tell someone else and then the whole world will know . . . What am I going to do??? Most of all, I was just plain scared.

I was still undergoing physical therapy for my back, and now I began to add HIV therapy to the regimen. Mostly I was just numbly going through the motions, not really doing anything, just existing. It wasn't long into the New Year before my punches, black eyes, and bruising began to become obvious. And of course, he was always sorry, oh so sorry. I didn't figure it would continue, but it did and it began to get progressively worse. Why do people stay in relationships like this? I only had to play the mantra that Joe had drilled into my head—"I love you, I'm so sorry, please don't leave me, I won't leave you, and oh by the way, did I tell you how much I love you?"

The wording began to change, and soon it was, "If you tell anyone, ANYONE, I will kill you, and maybe I'll even kill your daughter. Don't even think of us not being together."

How the hell, am I going to get out of this; or am I? Sometimes you are so afraid, you just do nothing. You take the path of least resistance and you become numb. But there is one thing I did and that was to send Marie, my thirteen year-old daughter, to go live with her dad. He lived in the same school district, and could make sure she got to school. Still recovering from my back injury, I couldn't drive her and there were no buses that came our way. I didn't realize it at the time, but this was a gift in disguise since she wasn't exposed to the violence. Still I'm sure she didn't believe the lies I told about how I got the bruises she was starting to notice. And no way did she know I had HIV.

Throughout my life I grew up with my mom saying, "Behind every dark cloud, there is a silver lining," and I lived my life with that saying driving me. There were always lessons to learn, and sometimes it took a long long time to find that lining. My kids used to tell me they were going to put it on my headstone when I died. So they grew up with it too! But it's the driving force behind my life, and it's also what got me through a lot of garbage, heartache, and finding the reason why I was going through this. After all, things like this don't happen to nice people, do they? I mean, not this? Right?

Chapter 2

Joe was on parole from prison when I first met him. I didn't know that for several weeks. One day he comes by my home and says," I have to go check in with my parole Officer, and I would really like him to meet you". A Parole Officer? What for? So Joe sits down and tells me his story of why he is on probation. He'd been selling black tar heroin back in 1989. He had lost his job, and knew he could make money at it. The way he told it sounded a lot different, but that was the gist of it. He got caught, was found guilty, went to prison in 1991 for 19 months and came out a changed man. So he said. And oh, by the way, he said, he never used it himself. Well, of course, I believed him. After all, I loved him, and people just don't lie about things like that, do they?

So at Joes encouraging, I went. Never in my life had I met someone on probation, little alone gone to meet their parole officer. I was introduced to this man, David Bowman, as Joe's girlfriend. For some reason he didn't have a smile on his face. More like a face that held, concern. I didn't know why. Most people we meet for the first time usually have some kind of a smile, but concern? Any way I was asked to wait in the waiting room while Joe went back to Bowman's office. About 10 minutes later, Joe was out of his office, and we said goodbye to Mr. Bowman, hum, still no smile. Maybe that's just the way parole officers are.

Looking back, I have no idea why I was so trusting and gullible. What was it in me that I needed a relationship with Joe so bad that I believed his words? Was he that good of a con artist, or was it me? Maybe I will find out later, hum.

It was around the first of the following year, in early 1993, that a man by the name of Richard Lasater, a Department of Corrections (DOC) officer, came by my house. This was Joe's new Parole officer. I invited him in. Richard said, "Well, I really need to talk to Joe, so how about we step outside for a minute". And about a minute had gone by and they were both in my living room.

Richard then had asked me point blank, "Has Joe informed you that he has Aids?" I replied with a stutter," A, yes he has." I didn't say when he told me, or how long we had been together. If I had volunteered that information, things would have most definitely turned out different. No one ever asked me those questions, and I didn't know enough to say, either.

Now Richard was a very hands-on DOC officer, and did a lot of what is called "field work," which means he did a lot of checking up on parolees out of the office. He asked if I had been tested for HIV and I told him that yes, I had, but I needed to have a follow-up test soon. And it was only a few weeks later that my test had come back positive. Why am I telling you about this guy? Because he and his wife, Rose, who was also a DOC officer, became my very best and closest friends, and still are to this very day. They have helped me through so much.

Richard showed up at the house a few days after my test results came back. I was home alone and he could tell by looking at me that I had gotten the results of my test and the news wasn't good. I fell into his arms and just started sobbing. Years later he would share with me he wished for and was looking for a reason to 'violate' Joe so he could send him back to prison to do all of his time. Looking back now, if this would have happened, it would have changed everything in my life. I have to say that I now know beyond any doubt that every event in life happens for a reason—even the most horrible, bad, and life-changing things. I needed to be walking into Joe's mom's kitchen that July day in 1993 and overhearing that conversation she was having with Joe's sisters . . . . Because that is when I knew that he had infected me with HIV on purpose.

Talk about a game changer. Joe never knew that I found out the truth from his mother, and she never knew I overheard the truth. Maybe she figured Joe had told me the truth. I even accompanied Joe to his doctors' appointments and no one there ever said "Oh by the way, did you know he has known for years? He has known for years he is HIV? Oh, and he really isn't just HIV . . . he has AIDs!!!" No, I wasn't to find out about all that for a while still.

It was the end of July of 1993 that I told Joe he had to leave, that I just couldn't live with him anymore. That I really had to focus on my physical therapy following my back injury; And his drinking was getting progressively worse as was the severity of my bruises, and people were starting to notice them more. Even my physical therapists were asking me about the bruises, and you can only make up so many lies, right?

He didn't leave without instilling in me the fact that he would kill me if I told anyone. "And I mean ANYONE! got it?" He would say over and over again. Each time a little different, but the same message. He would even threaten to kill my daughter. So I kept quiet for awhile. He would call several times a day and say, "just checking up on my favorite girl," or he would just drop in and say things like, "how you doing honey, and are you keeping quiet about our little secret?" It dawned on me that I just wasn't going to get rid of Joe, and I just didn't know what to do! I was frightened to death of what he was capable of doing, and was paralyzed with fear and all the 'what if's'. His mantra played over and over again in my head!

And then I got a call from my brother Mick! He wanted to know if he could move in with me and rent out the basement through the winter. Oh My God! What a gift this was. No way would Joe do anything to me or Marie with my brother here!

Mick worked in road construction and in our area that was seasonal work. He could save up some money for winter and help me out in the process. Perfect!!! Joe wouldn't ever lay another hand on me again! I still had to be very, very careful about my secret . . . "Shhhh, don't tell a soul! I will kill you and/or your daughter, shhh . . . I will be watching you, I can hide in the bushes around your house and you will never, never know!" The mantra played over and over continuously in my head, and I was afraid to say anything, to anyone. But I felt that at least if I kept my mouth shut, I would be safe. After all, my brother would protect me. There is no way he can or will hurt me now, is there?

So you wonder why people stay in horrible, painful, and destructive relationships? BECAUSE WE ARE SCARED TO DEATH FOR US AND OUR FAMILY!!! Without his money how am I going to pay my bills? Well it didn't take long before I was just a mess, and it was in September that

I reached a breaking point. This is also the time when I started crying . . . . I named it my crying time and it continued on for months and even years.

The crying time in September of 1993, started when I reached out for the very first time for help. It was just a phone call to a hotline of someone I would never know. I had a very difficult time talking and answering questions because I was crying, and crying, and crying. The National AIDS hotline has an amazing group of people; for let's face it, it had to be very difficult for that person to hear me and be able to glean the information necessary to help me. I probably should have been in a psych ward by now. Soon after I made that call, a woman at the Spokane AIDS Center called me, and later that day one of their representatives came out to see me. Someone was finally going to help me but there were some very hard decisions I was going to have to make, and I needed to make them very soon. *But I can't even think straight yet! I'm still crying!*

The Spokane AIDS Network took me under its wing and became a lifeline for me. They put me in touch with a sympathetic doctor who treated people with HIV/ AIDS and had the latest information and medications to help. The AIDS Network also put me in touch with a church that catered to the "infected and affected," and this was where I first met "gay people," as far as I knew. And even though I spent all my time in church crying, so many people would just stop and hug me or pass me their telephone number, saying, "Just call anytime, honey, and just talk if you need to, I'm a good listener." Well, I have to tell you I met the most loving and compassionate people, and there was not one judgment in sight! I didn't tell anyone about my secret yet, because it felt so good to get those hugs. And if I was to tell them any details, what if they didn't want me like Joe said. Realistically, they probably figured it out long before I finally told "my secret" one Sunday night several weeks later. And oh my god! They still hugged me and cared about me! They didn't care what it was—they were there for me—they accepted me for what I was, a woman infected with HIV, and they still hugged me! Ah ha! Well, Joe was wrong this time. Will there be other things that will play out to not be true?

Chapter 3

At church I met two wonderful women who were to play a very crucial role in my life. Sally was a pastor at this church, and Sharon was a parishioner who was gay—my first gay friend. Why is that important? Because it was the gay community which several months later gave me the strength and love I needed to help care for all of us who were knowingly infected by others, as well as the immense amount of basic courage it required because they were unable to do it for themselves.

When Pastor Sally heard my story, she was absolutely shocked. She sat through endless hours of my tears, and we would just work around them, no matter how long it took. She also put me in touch with Peter Frank, a wonderful, compassionate man who was the contact person at a retreat for people infected with HIV/AIDS, for five days . . . . free!!!

Pastor Sally was the one who had starting telling me that what had happened to me was a damn crime, and something should be done about it! One day after receiving another telephone threat from Joe about keeping my mouth shut and don't tell anyone, or else, I got to thinking . . . . the people at that church didn't leave me, and the people at the AIDS Network didn't kick me to the curb. Sharon just wanted to be my friend, someone to lean on, and my daughter Marie still loved me, and Sally kept saying that this was a crime.

So maybe, just maybe, I'm thinking and hoping, the police can really protect me and my daughter from Joe, because this situation just couldn't be allowed to continue. I was more afraid of him now than when he was living with me!

I had called this law Firm in the valley and made an appointment to talk to a John Clark. I ran my story through him, and he agreed that this was a police matter and gave me a name of a detective to contact. "Let me know what he says Susie, and maybe down the road we might be able to get you some compensation."

I called the police department and spoke briefly to a detective who made an appointment in a few days for me to come in and talk to a Detective Jimmy Jansen who would take an official report from me. Well, that sounded pretty good. At least now I could get some protection for Marie and me. Luckily my daughter never knew about the threats against her life, and well, my brother would be moving in soon. So I thought I was taking care of business, and naturally my crying continued through all of this. I asked Pastor Sally, who by now had become just Sally, to go with me "to keep me honest." And so a few days later Sally and I were headed to the Spokane Police Department to make a formal police request for protection. This was a day which would change not only my life, but the lives of thousands of people I would never know, by providing validation for them as infected people—people who never asked for the misfortune they had received, never deserved it, most importantly of all, weren't being "punished by God" for being gay—how many times do I have to say it? NOBODY DESERVES THIS UGLY, HORRIBLE DISEASE!! NOBODY !!!!

I didn't sleep well the night before my appointment at the Police Department. I was about to open Pandora's box, a real can of worms. However, I didn't really know that but I was fully aware that this was a turning point in my life as well as that of my family. I needed to tell my children (all of them) and my dad and brother soon and that just started me crying again. I felt like such a failure, so ashamed of myself that I even hooked up with someone like Joe. What was wrong with me? Why was I making such poor, embarrassing, and painful choices in my life? Worst of all, now it was not just me I was hurting but my whole family. Are they still going to be there for me? Are they going to say "Well, Susie, you really blew it this time, see ya!" After all, isn't that what Joe had said would happen? I really couldn't blame them if they did this. I had really screwed up my life now!!! Here I was forty-one years old, still suffering from my back injury from work, still on the L&I disability insurance, about to lose my home because I couldn't make the rent, and now on the verge of dropping a bombshell right in the middle of my life! What the hell was I thinking?

Chapter 4

"Look for the silver lining, Susie, the one behind this huge black cloud. It's there, honey, just keep looking." I could hear my mom say those words to me as clearly as if she were standing right there in front of me. She had been dead since March of 1992 but she was still very much present in my life spiritually. I kept thinking that I was glad she was on the other side because my latest situation would have killed her for sure. Oh, she would have been soooo disappointed in me; I was such a "people pleaser." I wouldn't have been able to live with her rejection of me, let alone take responsibility for her death! My mom and I were very close, and when she was dying of cancer she showed such overwhelming strength and acceptance. Even in the dying processes of life, she continued to teach me. We had set up a code, she and I, that when she got to the other side and was okay she would send me a message that would, beyond a shadow of doubt, make that clear.

About two months after mom died I was searching for a new place to move to. On the bulletin board at work one day I saw an ad posted for a two-bedroom house for rent, and it was close to work. I called the number listed. I went to look at it the following day. It was so cute. It looked as though it was in a park. The driveway was lined with shady trees and the yard was absolutely beautiful. I couldn't wait to see the inside. The older couple who had built this home had previously rented it out to families, and just wanted someone to take care of this place as if it were their own. Well, I told them, that was me. I was an excellent tenant and all the places I'd rented in the past were in much better condition when I moved out than when I had moved in. We were walking around to the back yard where I saw the most beautiful, huge, wild yellow rose bush. Wow! That was my mom's most favorite flower and I told Mr. and Mrs. Haynes about my mom just passing a short while ago, and that this was her favorite flower and that this must be an omen that I should take the house. Startled, they looked at each other and then back at me, and said, "You must be right, because that rosebush has always been pink!" I felt goosebumps raise on my arms and then I started laughing, Right then I knew mom had most definitely found a way to tell me she had made it safely to the other side and was here with me . . . .

Oh mommy, I have so screwed up my life. Please be with me as I am about to do something that I don't know if it's right or wrong, So I just did what I did best and just cried and cried and cried, and the more I cried the more I heard those familiar words, "behind every dark cloud is a silver lining." I didn't stop crying immediately, but now these were beginning to be happy tears, at least part of them were. I wasn't alone any more. She was with me. And I had received all the proof I needed of her presence when I saw the yellow rose bush that had always been pink before. And I had witnesses—Mr. and Mrs. Haynes, my new landlords.

Chapter 5

When morning finally arrived and it was time for me to get ready to jump off the edge of this cliff I had placed myself on, my face looked like someone had really worked me over, so as I had so often done lately, I just forget the makeup. Not even waterproof makeup was no longer effective against the ravages of my tears.

I remember sitting nervously in the police station, waiting for the detective to come out and get me. Sally was sitting there beside me, letting me know she was there for me and wouldn't leave my side, telling me over and over that I was strong and that this was the right thing to do, and I would be protected now.

Ahhhhh!! He just called my name. As I stood up I thought for sure I was going to throw up all over him, even though I couldn't tell you if I had eaten anything that morning or even the night before. He shook my hand and looked into my very red, swollen eyes already clouding over again with tears, as he patted my hand.

"Hello, Miss Wyatt. Did I say that right? Oh, good, I'm here to help you, so let's go into one of these rooms over here. It's quiet and safe, and you will have my full attention. Would you like something to drink?"

No sooner did we get into this "safe place" than I did what I did best—I burst immediately into a crying spell that lasted at least fifteen minutes. Then when I thought I had stopped, this wonderfully patient, kind man took my hand and quietly said to me, "You must have an awful lot of pain in you to cry like that. I am here for as long as it takes." I was finally able to sort of, more-or-less stop crying but it just never stopped for very long. I could only imagine how swollen my eyes were. They felt like they were growing tiny grains of sand under the lids.

I began to tell Detective Jimmy Jansen pretty much how the story of my life went from the first time I met Joe until today as I sat there in the safe room at the police station. I spilled out the whole sordid sequence of events that led me to be sitting here in front of him right now. This compassionate detective immediately became my hero, as well as my personal angel who not only was going to protect me and my daughter, but was going to blow the lid off the life I was living. Oh the power of secrets . . . .

It all started when I had a date with my oldest son, Donnie. This was a first for us, so I was pretty excited. I got off work at 11PM and was to meet him at a little neighborhood bar down the street from the hospital. I had just learned to shoot darts and was pretty good (must have been all those years I played baseball) and I was going to teach Donnie how to play. He actually showed up at the hospital where I worked and we left together. Boy, the place was really packed and several people I knew were there so I introduced my son to all of them, ordered a pitcher of beer, and we started playing darts with another couple, Doug and Diane. They immediately introduced us to Joe, a guy sitting at the table with them. I started talking to him when I wasn't shooting darts and he seemed like a pretty nice person. Not really handsome, but not bad looking either. Well, before we knew it (how time flies when you are having fun) the night was ending, the bar was closing for the night, and my son had caught onto darts pretty fast.

And Joe asked me out on a date. Wow, now that was pretty cool, I thought. We felt somehow connected, especially when we discovered his mom was a nurse at the same hospital where I worked. What a small world, I thought. My days off were Friday and Saturday and back to work Sunday at 3 PM. When we were leaving I noticed he was riding a motorcycle and he asked me if I rode. I laughed and said I had only been on my brother's Gold Wing a few times,

Friday night was rolling around and I was sure glad I was wearing jeans because he showed up at the house on his bike with an extra helmet for me. Joe told me to put my arms around him and hang on. Now I know why guys like chicks on their bikes. I didn't date very much so the attention Joe showed me was really feeling pretty good. We went and played darts with some friends of his and then went to dinner and back again to play more darts. The night came to an end with some really good kisses. He asked for my phone number, and said goodnight at the front door. And that was how my relationship with Joe started. I was swept off my feet. He called every day, said he was going to be out of town the following weekend but set up a date for when he got back.

I was floating at work all week, and come Thursday when I arrived at work there was a vase of gorgeous flowers waiting for me with a card saying he missed me and would see me soon . . . . WOW, well, that had never happened to me before. Man, I thought, this guy must really like me, because I was sure falling for him. I was in a place in my life where I had a pretty good job, lived in a really cute house, my daughter was thirteen, and doing okay as far as teenagers go, and I was healing emotionally from the loss of my mom.

When Joe showed up for our second date he was driving a car and we went to dinner, then dancing, and out to play darts. Well, this night never ended, and our sex was fantastic. Safe sex never came up and when he asked me later on about whether he should have used a condom, I told him that I had been "fixed," and that was the extent of our conversation about safe sex. I couldn't get pregnant and he was okay with that. It wouldn't be until a few months later that the reality of that conversation would smack me in the face when Joe was in the hospital with pneumonia, and he told me he just learned he had HIV. Oh My God! Could I have this? I had gone to the doctor's office several days before this with the flu, and found out later down the road that this was one of the major signs of early HIV infections. My doctor kept excellent records and we were able to use this in court as to exactly when I became infected. And then not long after that, I had my accident at work. That is when Joe moved in with me and it wouldn't be until July of the following year when the ugly truth of how I became infected started to unravel, sort of like taking a sweater apart and seeing how crinkly the yarn is.

My daughter moved in with her dad in September 1992 so she could attend a particularly good junior high school, and Joe moved in with me. I had met a man by the name of Dean Bowman while Joe was in the hospital. He was Joe's DOC Parole Officer . . . . What? Yep! Another bomb shell. And another synchronicity. By now I was more concerned about my health, (I could possibly have contracted HIV by now; I'd suffered a major back injury; had only half my normal income to live on; was going to physical therapy three times a week; taking drugs for the pain). Yep! I have really screwed up my life. When Joe told me he'd been in prison for selling, black tar heroin, but came out a changed man—well, of course I believed him. He was so wonderful to me and if I did have HIV, well it was an accident, wasn't it? Nobody would ever infect anybody on purpose, would they? My life was falling apart, but Joe was there for me, he wouldn't leave me . . . . This is how "grooming of a victim by a predator" started—promises of unconditional love, they will never leave you, or you will never leave them, threatening you, building a fear factor in you that also brought about the physical abuse, and bruises that started me into covering up for him; and then throw in the drinking and needless to say, well, my life became very volatile, and I was frightened to death.

Two hours later, I am leaving Detective Jimmy Jensen's safe room, my eyes so swollen from crying that I needed sunglasses just to walk inside the building. He told me he would check out a few things and I could expect to hear from him in a couple of weeks, and, by the way, I should file for a "protection order". Are you serious? If he finds out, I am dead meat, or my daughter is! No, oh that's right, she is at her dad's. Okay, she is safe. But I'm not. Don't you understand? He can hide in my yard, watch me, attack me anytime if he finds out!!!!!!

I did end up filing for a protection order but not until a few days later, on Friday afternoon. I remember telling the judge to please remember my name, and if I came up dead to please know that it would be murder!! I think the judge was convinced that I needed the protection because after he had read the reason for this order he asked me several questions, voicing his concern for me, and suggested I immediately find another place to stay for a while. Which is exactly what I did.

Chapter 6

I had signed up to go to a retreat for people infected with HIV/AIDS, and Peter Frank, one of its directors, had taken me through the complete evaluation required to be accepted for this very special retreat where I would learn all the latest information regarding medications and treatment. There were also several other classes available to take if I chose. There were many different kinds of crafts you could learn to do, but most importantly, I would meet others who were infected, and see how they were living with this overwhelming problem. There would also be lots and lots of fantastic food, nutritious meals prepared and donated by one of the nearby local high-end restaurants. I would also have a private room and several nurses and a doctor were on hand in case one was needed. Wow! This sounded like it was going to be just what I needed.

Knowing that my brother, Mickey, would be moving into my rented home while I was gone, I felt an immediate sense of relief. Now not only could I go some place safe for several days but equally as importantly, I would feel safe returning home, too. Now maybe I could focus on finding that silver lining behind this big black cloud, and get on with my life. I had to tell my brother about my HIV, for his own protection, and you know what? He didn't walk out of my life, he didn't kick me to the curb, he didn't berate me for being so stupid. No, he didn't do any of those things that Joe said he would. He just simply loved me. Although he really wanted to kill Joe, I mean really! Kill him! It took a very long talk and a real promise that he wouldn't carry out his wish. I remember telling Mickey that was too easy a way out for Joe, and that I wanted him to die with this disease just like me. Also, getting rid of him wasn't worth going to prison for. I couldn't bear the thought of losing my brother, too. Mickey was the first family member I had confided in, and he was still family,

Whew, I was so glad I hadn't lost him. We had always been close growing up, and when I told him about going on this retreat and the hope that maybe I would find a silver lining for all of this, he just hugged me and said, "You know Susie, only you would say that, and only someone like you will find it. I love you, sis."

I told my daughter, Marie, over the weekend, and we just cried the whole time. It seemed as though every time I thought about what I was putting her through I would burst into tears, and I would think about how my mom died and now I was going to put this beautiful little girl through my own dying process. Who was going to be there for her? I was so guilt-ridden I just couldn't stop crying, but I knew I had to stop for her sake! She couldn't see me falling apart all the time—what kind of message is that sending her? It would send her the message that I really messed up my life and hers, too, along with the question of how people would treat her when they find out her mother had—you know—that disease that only prostitutes, drug addicts, and gay people get!!!! And you know, it's contagious; it jumps off people so stay away from Marie, she probably has it too. This is not something I made up, that's exactly what people were not only saying, but really believed . . .

In September of 1993, I had a yard sale to earn some extra money for my bills, when a man walked up and introduced himself. Jack was his name and he and his wife Gayle had just moved into the neighborhood. They were potters who made their own pottery and sold it around the Pacific Northwest at trade shows. This sounded really interesting because I already knew a little about ceramics, and this seemed as though it couldn't be too much different. Maybe, I thought, they could use my help or something.

Jack and Gayle became my guardian angels, and what a lifeline they were. On our very first meeting in their pottery shop I broke down and told them of my HIV status and the story of how I became infected. They became another set of eyes to protect me. I immediately became a daily fixture in their shop doing everything except throwing pottery and lifting the boxes. It became my lifeline and I spent countless time there just helping out in any way I could. This really became my therapy. I was overjoyed to have something constructive to do outside my home, and they were only two houses away. Gayle became my best friend and confidante. When I was getting ready for my retreat, it was Gayle who invited Marie to stay with her and Jack, and "play" in the shop while I was gone.

On Sunday afternoon Gayle and Marie were helping me pack for my big week ahead. At the same time Mick was moving in some of his stuff, when there was a knock at my door. It was Detective Jimmy Jenson. What in the world was he doing at my house? Maybe he just wanted to see where I lived and how I lived. You know, make sure I was not some "fly-by-night hooker" or something like that. No, that wasn't the reason at all, He had stopped by to let me know that Joe was in the process of being served a no-contact order, and just with what he had learned from his investigation so far, he felt he should share the information; that maybe I should go someplace safe for the night since I was leaving in the morning anyway. No sooner did those words come out of his mouth, the phone rang. OH God! It was Joe! At least I thought so. Only two words were said and it was like a whisper, "You're dead!!" I slammed down the phone and immediately burst into tears. Even though Detective Jansen was there in the room I couldn't swear that it was Joe. Maybe it was someone else. Yeah, right! Who?? But being the honest person I was and the fact that the message was whispered, maybe he had gotten someone else to call . . . . I couldn't swear it was Joe.

Quickly I finished packing, and so did Marie, while Detective Jimmy made a few phone calls and talked to my brother. We went to Gayle's home for the night and left early the next morning. I dropped Marie off at school and headed straight for the retreat. I was definitely in need of a safe place and some rest and relaxation. Where, oh, where was I going to find that silver lining? Or who would I find? Could it be Jack and Gayle? Or maybe Pastor Sally or Detective Jansen? Or my brother? Or was I going to find it within myself? If I had known at the time what lay ahead I might have never come back . . . .

When I pulled up in front of the Bozarth Center, I felt as though I was entering one of those fancy spa resorts. You know the kind that you would have to hit the lottery to afford to go to! I thought I must be at the wrong place. There must have been a dumb-founded look on my face because a man standing on the porch asked, "Are you here for the retreat? Good. Well, come on in. I'm Peter Frank; are you Susie? So glad you could make it. There are several people here who are excited to meet you, but first let's get you registered."

The moment I walked in I totally froze. I looked around in a state of shock at a room that was absolutely beautifully furnished!!! But that wasn't what stopped me in my tracks, it was the people!

"It's okay, Susie, they're here for the same reason you are," Peter said. I looked at him and asked, "Do they all have HIV?" Well, the answer was yes, and it turned out that they were in the several different stages of this terrible disease. I saw some in wheelchairs, some with I.V. poles; some with what looked like large, ugly bruises on their skin. They were in their pajamas and robes. OH MY GOD!!! Is that what I'm going to look like in a few years? So I did what I did best, and broke down into tears that were to continue daily throughout my time at this retreat.

I met some amazing people there; I mean some really awesome people. They were definitely in the angel department, and the staff at this retreat fell into that same category. The retreat was called aptly enough "Strength for the Journey," and it was completely supported financially by the United Methodist Churches in all the states that I have lived in. Thank you for all they do, just doesn't cut it; there's so much more that I wish I could tell them. They not only dried my many tears during my stay there as well as over the following years but they gave me the strength to go forward on a tumultuous journey that I wasn't even aware I was on. And that old saying that there is strength in numbers is really true.

I had never been around gay people before, at least not that I knew of, and to my surprise I found them to be just like regular people. They cried, too. They hurt like me, and they laughed as I did, and they were full of information as well as some of the many pitfalls to watch out for. They also pointed me to the doctors in Spokane who treated "the infected". This was something my doctor was encouraging me to do, because, this wasn't his specialty. He was one doctor who above all wanted the VERY BEST treatment possible for me.

There were several "release" discussion groups at the retreat. When the residents heard how I became infected and what I was about to do—file charges against Joe for infecting me—they were all solidly behind me. I never expected that. What I heard from them was: "You go girl! You can do it! Do it for all of us who were infected the same way you were, and because we are GAY everybody thinks we deserve it! Do it for us! And we'll be right by your side! DO IT FOR ALL OF US BECAUSE NO ONE DESERVES THIS HORRIBLE DISEASE." Oh boy, I had no idea what I was getting myself into!

I met Pastor Tom who was the big honcho of this group and who was instrumental in getting me involved in public speaking. Yep, that's right, and I didn't know it then, but I was to find myself speaking in many different forums on many different occasions.

Three other women were at this retreat, and not all of the men there were gay. It was quite a variety of people. One woman in particular that Peter Frank wanted me to meet was Lynn. She was not only an eight-year survivor but she was able and willing to help me navigate through a maze of information. She showed me where to go for different kinds of help, such as doctors; what all the different medications were; and if there was a problem with insurance, what organization could provide help; what times of the month to go and get free food; where to get vouchers for gas—she was a treasure trove of information. Lynnie and I became very good friends and remained close right up to the very end which would not be for another nine years, when she finally passed in her sleep, and pain free. Her journey here was over. We were quite a powerhouse when we did public speaking together. But that wasn't to be for a while. There were still a couple more bombshells to go off in my life.

Chapter 7

When I was a young child, my brother, my sister, and our mom spent a great deal of time in a small town called LaCross, Washington. That was where my mom and dad grew up and where my Grandma and Grandpa Malby lived, as well as several aunts who were our playmates, considering my mom was the oldest of eleven children. Grandpa worked for the railroad and he and grandma lived in what was called "the section house" because it was right beside the railroad tracks. I have many wonderful memories of those times, but this special one has carried through all my life.

Everyone else was gone this particular day and I was in the kitchen with grandma. A stranger came to the back door asking for work and said that he would be more than happy if she had some food to spare in payment. Now this was around 1960, long before homeless people stood on a corner with a sign saying, "Will work for food," or others asking, "Can you spare some change?" He ended up weeding the garden, which was no small job! No sir, back then you canned everything you could, and considering there were still five kids at home, a big garden was a necessity. Living in the city like we did, I thought grandma was crazy, letting a stranger, actually back then we called them bums, so close.

Concerned about our safety, I warned, "He could be a killer or something, grandma!"

Grandma just laughed and said, "Honey, you just never know when that might be Jesus in disguise."

"Or jewels in your crown, right?" I asked her.

"This is a little different, Susie," was her calm response.

This is the only time in my life I can remember that grandma and I sat down together, with no interruptions,and she taught me what "Jewels In My Crown" was all about. And I didn't know until many years later when I started on this journey of my spiritual path how important this simple phrase would become. The best thing about it is how good it feels to acquire so many full circles in your life and you discover the jewels without even knowing it!

"Well, Susie, let's see, where to begin. Young or old, it doesn't matter.Sometimes you just feel the need to do something for somebody, not because of your own pride—now remember 'pride goes before a fall'; but because you just want to do it. And you're not expecting anything in return. If you can do that something and they don't know who did it, well that's even better; that's a jewel in your heavenly crown that will be placed on your head when you go to heaven. Also, honey, when you get older you'll have a past you can look back on." I remember clearly that was one of the few times grandma laughed out loud. I hadn't heard anything funny, but oh well, old people were like that sometimes. She continued, "You will notice that there is a beginning and then an end, and you can see how far you have come and what you have learned from this experience. And always in your life, look for that silver lining and when you have found it, well then, honey, you not only have come full circle, but you have also acquired a jewel in your crown." I have since learned that another name for those full circles are "life lessons," and they could sometimes be quite painful, last a long, long time, and never forgotten. Thanks Gramma for the info, and it has played an important part of my life ever since

On our last day at this amazing retreat, we held a group gathering and,with all of us seated in a circle, we were asked what we had learned, what we could apply to our everyday life, and which person had made a positive impression here, and what you had learned from them. Here are some of the things that I learned and would remain with me to this day:

#1—I was not alone

#2—I was loved

#3—Don't let fear control you or the future

#4-Ask for help!!! This was very difficult for me to do, but I would learn very quickly what a lifeline this would become.

#5-You can have a very long and good life even when you live with this disease. This was the most important thing I took away from this Strength for the Journey retreat because I learned I wasn't going to die tomorrow! I had met people who were seventeen years a survivor, and they kept saying there would be new medications soon that would extend our lives even more.

During our discussions, many people had talked about returning to the real world. This was kind of a heads-up for me, at this time when all these warm and fuzzy feelings from the retreat came crashing down around me. You will need to put all those things you just learned into practice a lot sooner than you thought, they reiterated. Well, they weren't wrong.

Chapter 8

The first thing I did when I got home Sunday afternoon was share with my daughter and Jack and Gayle, my pottery friends, all the cool things I'd learned at the retreat. Boy, was I flying high! And perhaps best of all was the knowledge that I wasn't going to die tomorrow! And that there really was hope. Okay, so let's start looking for that silver lining. Three days later I would start on these medications that were going to do that.

Antiretroviral medications are a combination of drugs that would hinder the virus from many different angles—by slowing down the damage to my CD4 and CD8 cells that were targets for the virus. These medications would help block the virus from invading my cells and replicating itself. Yes, I really learned a lot about this invader, this destroyer of life, but no one had prepared me for the awful sickness and nausea caused by the medications, and oh, my God, was I ever sick. It would take years before I would be on medications that weren't either killing me or making me sick. There were times that most of the drugs I was on were side-effect medications to counter the toxicity of the ones I was taking to help slow down the progression of the disease. We wouldn't find out until several months later that my prescription for AZT was miss written and over-dosed me by twice the amount. Geez, no wonder I was sicker than a dog!

This really played into the physical therapy I was undergoing for my back. Because of the overwhelming nausea every day I had cancelled several sessions and was now being threatened that if I didn't show up for scheduled appointments my disability monies would be cut off and I would be on my own financially. At the time I'd still kept it a secret as to why I was so sick because Joe had told me never, never, tell them because the liability and industry insurance would drop me like a hot potato! So I went to my therapy sessions whether I was throwing up or not, and this was almost more than I could handle, but I had to get better, because I needed the money! Please, just let me get better so I can go back to work, that's where I want to be I was struggling to just pay the basics. I had food stamps and ate over at Gayle's a lot and that really helped. But I had to forget about things like car insurance, cable TV, or my power bill. Do people with this HIV go back to work? Can they work? Maybe if my back gets better I might.

A week after the retreat, I got a phone call from Detective Jansen asking me if I could come in Tuesday and go over the results of his investigation. He mentioned that there would be a prosecutor there too by the name of Jay Sweets. Okay, that sounded fine to me. Not being fully aware of what was really going on, I picked up my friend, Pastor Sally, and arrived as at my 10 am appointment with no idea of the bombs that would soon be exploding.

It was a beautiful fall day, the kind of weather we live for here in Spokane, with the trees changing in all their amazing palette of colors and the smell of the changing weather in the air. This would have been a good day to simply escape the problems of everyday life and just stroll along the centennial trail that followed the river which ran from Idaho all the way through downtown Spokane and tumbled down the falls that were absolutely amazing in daylight, but were lit up at night. Yes, this would definitely have been the perfect time to take off life and just wallow in the beauty of the glorious autumn weather, and forget everything that was going on in my life. But I didn't do that, I went to my appointment, and as they say, "the rest is history.' Oh Boy . . . .

Detective Jansen was waiting for us inside the police station, and he walked us over to an office area that was enclosed with glass. There was a locked security area we had to pass through just to enter the office. Wow, what is this all about? My life as I knew it was just about to explode and I didn't even know it . . . .

Sally was asked to remain out in the waiting room, and as I looked back uncertainly at her she just smiled and said, "It's okay, you can do this." I was introduced to a very tall man, a little on the thin side, with piercing blue eyes and sandy-colored hair. He was a nice-looking man wearing a suit that looked as though it belonged at the cleaner's for a pressing job. He shook my hand and asked me if I would like something before we got started. Started? The first thing he asked me was if I knew why I was here and how had I found my way to Detective Jansen.

"I was asked to come in to go over the stuff that Detective Jansen has found in his investigation of Joe, the man who knowingly infected me with HIV. And to answer your second question, John Clark and Jim Delmonico, civil attorneys, had told me when I talked to them first that what I had told them was criminal, and to contact the police department and ask to talk to Jimmy Jansen to start looking into Joe's past," I responded.

"So it was after you met with Detective Jansen that you were advised to file a restraining order on Joe or any of his family, is that correct?" He asked.

"Yes.".

"And have you had any problems from this Joe guy?" He continued.

"No," I said. "But my brother is living with me now. I have been getting a lot of strange phone calls, though".

"Do you know anybody at Valley Hospital who might be calling from there and threating you?"

"Well, Joe's mom is a nurse there, but she wouldn't do that. I work there but I have been on L&I from a back injury for over a year. I have lots of friends there but no one that I can think of that would want to call me and threaten me or like I said, just some hang-ups or breathing and whispering things that I really can't understand. Do you think Joe is doing this?"

The prosecuting attorney and the detective answered at the same time, "Yes."

I kind of had the feeling at this point I wasn't going to like the rest of this conversation.

"Susie, here are just a few things that we have found so far in this investigation. Are you okay?" This doesn't sound good I thought to myself and I could feel some color leave my face.

"Yea, I'm okay, I think." Was my response.But deep down inside I wasn't so sure.

"First, Joe was convicted of selling black tar heroin, and sent to prison for thirteen months, a very light sentence. Do you know why? Because he had used his HIV status to get his sentence reduced downward because of his health. So this meant that since there was a public record of his HIV status he was not entitled to privacy. Part of his probation was he had to inform anyone he was having sex with that he had HIV and would use protection. And you had said you weren't told till September 23rd when Joe was in the hospital, right? And you had been with Joe sexually since you had met him in July, correct?"

At this point I was feeling rather sick, but I managed to say, "Yes, that is all true."

"Susie, we need you to sign some release forms so we can check your medical records. They might tell us when you became infected." "Oh, and by the way, do you know of any other women he might have been with?"

OH MY GOD! I hadn't even thought of that but the answer was yes. All the color had drained from my face. I could feel it and both of these two men had noticed, too. Obviously concerned for my well-being and aware of the obvious stress I was under, they asked me if I was okay and suggested that maybe I should have something to drink.

Yes, it was quite possible I wasn't the only one he had infected with this deadly disease which really had no cure in sight. It wasn't until much later that I discovered one of these other women was the mother of two children who hadn't found out until she read about this case in the Seattle Times. They not only were looking for her but now Joe was being charged with premeditated murder. It was a precedent case for Washington State to charge someone deliberately going around infecting unsuspecting people. I had no idea of the Pandora's box that was about to be opened.

Detective Jansen also informed me that the Department of Corrections parole officer should have let me know of Joe's HIV the minute I had met him. I had attended a meeting with Joe very shortly after we had gotten together. There I met an Officer David Bowman who was young, maybe around twenty-six, about 5'7, with short brown hair. Joe had introduced me as his girlfriend, mentioning that I worked at the same hospital as his mom; and that's where we met—wasn't that cool, man, like it was meant to be!" I remember Joe's words vividly. But wait, we had met in a bar, I thought to myself, hum. I was asked to stay out in the waiting room and Joe and Officer Bowman went into a back room. About fifteen minutes later Joe came out and we left. I didn't know it at the time, but this bit of info was to play a pivotal part in the justice arena later down the road.

"Susie," Jimmy said, "everything you've shared with me has checked out, but now we need some solid proof, and that is harder to obtain. So now we need to obtain subpoenas for your medical records, and Joe's Department of Corrections records and hospital records. And by the way, it might be a good idea to carry a weapon with you at all times. We have good reason to suspect that he was in Montana recently trying to buy a gun. And you need to know where your daughter is at all times."

Oh shit! Needless to say, my face went back to a white shade and I felt a little light-headed. Oh, man, I think I am going to faint, which I immediately did! Several minutes later, I recovered enough to continue.

Mr. Sweet had warned that this was going to be a very difficult case to prove and asked whether I might have anything in my background that could be problematic in a court of law. He reiterated that I was going to be investigated thoroughly and that he would need to know any possible derogatory information before he started to put time into this.

"Not that I can think of," was my response. "I was just a regular white, single mom, dated a little, worked hard, well, until my injury, wasn't into drugs—well, maybe a little pot—didn't drink a lot, had a few beers when I went out to play darts. I felt I had a pretty good reputation with lots of friends and I spent a lot of time with Jack and Gayle in the pottery shop. You know, pretty solid that is until all of this."

Two hours later, I emerged from the prosecutor's office with Detective Jansen, and rejoined Sally.

"I will contact you in about a month and let you know where we are. In the meantime be careful and alert. Call if anything is scaring you or you feel on edge, okay? Here is my home phone number, Susie. I mean it! Call anytime."

Okay, so now I am wondering, what have I just gotten my daughter and myself into? Thank God I had my brother living with me . . . .

Sally was staring at me and it wasn't until we were outside and sitting on a bench in the shade that I broke down in tears and said, "Oh, Sally, I'm so scared, what have I done?" I went over everything that had taken place in the prosecutor's office and learning of the information that they had discovered, which explained the color, or lack thereof, on my face. We had planned to go out to lunch after this meeting but considering what I had just found out about Joe, well, let's just say it would have been a waste of money. I didn't know if it was the effect of the stress I was under, or the new medications my new doctor had placed me on—either way, I had no appetite. Food was the last thing I wanted to think about.

My new doctor was Susan Cophner, and she shared an office with Joe's doctor, which I didn't know until one day as I was signing in I noticed his name on the sheet, and suddenly I was scared to death! The nurse called me into the room immediately and we found out that yes, Joe's new doctor was here and that Joe had been here for an office visit but was finished and gone. My doctor and her staff made sure that to the best of their ability, this would never happen again. They knew about how I became infected and by whom. Whew!!! I felt like I had just dodged my first bullet! All this fear and stress I was suffering was just from me filing a protection order. What was going to happen if and when the prosecutor filed charges against him? Oh boy!

Chapter 9

Dr. Cophner was concerned about my health and current lab work which showed her that my latest blood counts were not looking good. When referring to my counts I'm talking about my CD4 and CD8 T-cells. Those are what are called "helper cells" and they are the ones in our systems that produce cells to fight infections—sort of like calling in the army to make sure everything in our bodies is running okay. What the HIV virus does is find a way to insert itself into the CD4 helper cells, changes the DNA of those cells to think that the invading virus is really one of them. Then it ends up replicating itself and spews itself out into our bodies and does as much damage as it can until the good helper cells find them and kill them off. The front lines are always changing as they travel throughout the body and with the helper cells in a life-and-death battle, well, let's just say, the lower my CD4 cell count is, the lower my health is. The higher my CD8 cells are means a higher degree of infection present, and the HIV virus attacks where it detects a weakness. It could be your kidneys, lungs, bones, skin cancer or cancers of any kind, strange infections or even dementia, which is the deterioration of the brain. Alzheimer's disease is a form of this, and for some reason this is found in many people with advanced stages of AIDS, as well as what is called "wasting syndrome".

My counts were in the area which tells the doctors to start me on medications to begin battling the virus and the first drug they placed me on was called AZT. That's when I became very sick from the medication and ended up on several other drugs to fight the side-effects of the AZT. For a person who had a hard time even taking Tylenol, what! Was this a joke! It was several months later that we would discover the prescribed dosage was twice what it was supposed to be, and it affected my stomach and throat to this day. The regimen of medications would change constantly and it wouldn't be for many years that we would find the right combination of meds that would begin giving me a quality of life that I could live with.

My doctor and I had just chalked up my being so ill was due to the stress I was under and that, yes, AZT can make you feel very sick on its own. And the stress I was under wasn't helping either so let's put you on another pill to help with the stress. Well, why not, I thought. I was already taking a handful. What's one more!

Lunch with Sally was definitely out, and after I told her some of the things the detective had found out, she wasn't very hungry either. When I got home I had about an hour before I had to pick up Marie from school, so I went to the pottery shop and started putzing around and telling Jack and Gayle about the meeting and that I would find out in about a month or so what to do.

Gayle said, "Susie, do you know what a precedent case is?"

"Well, not really, but I guess I'll find out soon, right?" I said.

I picked Marie up after school and took her over to her dad's place so she could gather up some clothes she had left there. She was going to stay with me for a while. Her dad was going to be working out of town for about a month, and Marie didn't get along with her stepmother, so she was excited to be coming home. This was a good time for Marie and me to sit down and have a long talk about all that had happened in our lives. I couldn't seem to overcome the shame and guilt that I felt and now I'd be putting her through it. Where the hell is that silver lining? Sadly, I wouldn't find it for a very long time . . . .

I am amazed my little girl is so strong and loves me so much. She was definitely what kept me focused, and kept telling me that I had to stop Joe from hurting anyone else. And she was right, but now I had to go tell my dad. Thursday morning I took Marie to school and headed over to my dad's place for morning coffee. Dad knew something was wrong as soon as I walked into the house and said something to the effect of, "So what's the matter, honey?" I find even with my own kids I know how to read them. I guess it's no different regardless of how old we are.

So with coffee in hand I told my father the details of what had happened and what I was doing as far as filing charges against Joe. My dad was so angry, that just like my brother, I had to make him promise not to kill Joe or possibly even have someone he knew kill him. We needed to see what the prosecutor was going to do. It was very rare that any of us kids ever saw our dad cry, but that morning we both had a crying time with my dad holding me tight, telling me how much he loved me and that I needed to do this, and he would stand by me all the way. I had asked him if it was okay to use my maiden name to protect my children and he agreed that it was a good idea. And so I started to educate him as to what I knew about HIV. But then I started crying all over again, because back then this dreaded disease was a quick killer, and a person really didn't have a lot of time to live, maybe five to ten years at the best. A few hours later I leave my dad's home and head for my physical therapy, looking like a Mack truck had hit me.

Well, I told myself, my dad hadn't thrown me out of the house. He had even said that he loved me and would stand by me. Maybe Joe was wrong about everything as far as the reactions to my telling people that I had HIV. At least my family was there for me and my friends, Jack and Gayle, and my other friend James.

James and I worked together at the hospital, although in different fields. He was a wonderful, kind person. His longtime girlfriend was dying of multiple sclerosis, and he worked full-time at the hospital and took care of her at home until she passed. We became good friends, and when I stopped by to see him one day about a week after she died, he was trying to sort through her possessions that were to be given away. I spent the next several hours with him, helping him through this painful task, and wondered how my kids and family would go through my things. So I did what I do best, and just collapsed and cried, finally telling James about having HIV, and how frightened I was and wondering what was I going to have to go through. James didn't back away from me, he just grabbed me, hugged me, and said, "I will be there, Susie. You won't be alone and neither will Marie." He was definitely a caregiver. He was my first friend from work that I told. James was also suffering a great loss and being together we could more or less take each other's pain away and focus on someone else's. James had taken time off from work so we made a date to go down to a small town south of Spokane on Saturday. There was to be a craft and art sale and it would give us a fun day off from life. I was taking my daughter over to her brother's new place so she could spend the day with her big brother. I wasn't sure what they were going to be doing but they were both looking forward to it.

Chapter 10

Donnie and his girlfriend, Lyn, had just moved into a new place together. She had two small children, Donna who was 4 and LeAnn who was 18months old. I had met her a few times and wasn't crazy about her. I just felt there was something weird about her, but Donnie seemed to be in love with her and happy. I hadn't told him about my situation, and this day wasn't the right time. It was Marie's and Donnie's day, and I certainly didn't want to ruin it. If Marie wanted to talk to him about it I told her that was okay with me. Marie said she probably wouldn't because she just wanted to forget the whole thing for a while too.

I spent some time with Donnie and his ready-made family. Two things were obvious right away—the stairs in the house and the fact that LeAnn, the 18-month-old baby had two black eyes!!!

While Donnie had been out watering the yard a few days ago, Donna, the 4-year-old, had come out to tell him that LeAnn had fallen down the stairs. She was crying and Donnie picked her up and she seemed okay, but how did she get up the stairs? Well, it turned out that Donna had taken her little sister up the stairs, and then fell. When Lyn got home from a class she was taking at the YWCA, Donnie thought they should take LeAnn to the hospital and have her checked out to make sure she was all right. However, Lyn told him that she would be okay, that they would just watch her and see how she was in the morning, and if need be Lyn would take her to the doctor in the morning.

Other than the black eyes she had by the time the next morning arrived, she seemed fine. But Donnie still felt she should see the doctor. Lyn said she would take her in in the afternoon, and Donnie left for work. When he got home from work that night, Lyn told him that the doctor said she was fine.

By the time I saw LeAnn she looked like a little raccoon, and there was now a guard on the stairs. Hmm . . . Did Donna really have it in her to push her little sister down the stairs, and did she know what a bad thing that was? Donnie had said that she was the only one in the house, and that, "She is kind of strange, mom. She has to have all the attention all the time and it's like her and Lyn are fighting for my attention." Yeah, her and her mom! "And when I pick up 'my lil weeble-wabble' (leAnn's nickname) she just hangs on for dear life. Maybe that will change over time, but for now it sure is weird," Donnie had said, and I had agreed with him. I let Donnie know what my plans for the day were and that I should be home by 4 o'clock, and he said he would have Marie home maybe around 7 o'clock.

As if we'd ordered it, there were gorgeous blue skies and plenty of sunshine—a perfect time to spend with a good friend in a quaint little town, enjoying this day of food, music and crafts. What a nice day James and I had. It had been a long time since either one of us had laughed. Little did I know I was about to have another bombshell dropped in my life. Geez! When are these going to stop? I was beginning to feel like my life was a war zone and there weren't any silver linings in sight.

Soon after I arrived home, the phone rang and it was Lyn, Donnie's girlfriend, calling from a hospital in Spokane. All she would say was there had been an accident and Donnie wanted me to come as soon as possible. Lyn wouldn't tell me anything . . . . Was it Marie? Was it Donnie? She still refused to give me any details even after I yelled at her, so out the door I went. I would deal with her later—I was really mad that she wouldn't tell me what had happened!

Baby LeAnn was in the hospital in critical condition, and the doctors were saying this was abuse! Donnie was beside himself, crying and really shaken up. But what was really strange was that Lyn was much more concerned that Donnie, her boyfriend, was so upset, than over the fact that her own little baby lying in a hospital bed in the CCU unit, not expected to live. What the hell was going on? What was wrong with this woman? I kept thinking that none of this was fitting, something wasn't right. Then I found out that Lyn never did take LeAnn to the doctors. When question by me, she was just silent. Never talking at all. And still no emotion, no tears, no nothing!

Lyn's brother was staying with them and he was at home with Donna and Marie. So I left to go get Marie and take Donna home with me. We were in the process of packing up some things for Donna when Child Protection Services showed up to take Donna into their care. Anytime there is a suspicion of abuse they are called in, so I could understand that. What I couldn't get my head around was that it had to be from her fall down the stairs? Right? I didn't think that was abuse but instead a very bad and terrifying accident. I let Lyn's brother know that he should call his parents who lived in northern Oregon, and let them know what was happening. I remember him saying, "Oh, they won't care, but I'll call." What! They wouldn't care? That was their grandbaby? What is going on in this family?"

That night Leanne died, and Lyn was arrested. We were all dumb-founded, and even though we were not blood relatives, we paid for a funeral for this special little baby, and I remember Lyn showing up for it with two policemen escorting her. She was in full shackles and dressed in an orange jumpsuit. Well! No doubt about her being a prisoner . . . . and still no tears! Now I understand that people sometimes react differently when under stress or in shock, but really? She showed no emotion, and was just very stoic.

Donnie came over to my home to stay that night. He said it was too difficult to be in the house all by himself, well, I would think so.

The next morning I got up around 7 o'clock, turned on the morning TV news only to hear that there was an APB out for my son! And if anyone saw him or his car, they were to call the Spokane police immediately. Oh MY GOD!!! So I called an attorney I knew and was really surprised that not only did he answer the phone but that his office was open. I explained to Berney Nalley what was going on and he said to bring Donnie to his office right away, and that is what we did. Later that day, Donnie was arrested and charged with second-degree murder for Leann's death.

All of us, being Donnie's family and friends, were totally shocked by this. Of all people, this was not him. Donnie loved kids, and they loved him. We used to call him "the pied piper" because children were somehow always drawn to him. And it wasn't a surprise that Donnie would hook up with a woman with children, but none of us suspected abuse and murder of a baby that he loved as his own. It only made sense that Lyn would say that Donnie had caused LeAnn's death. This could easily be proven wrong, right? We were positive that Donnie was innocent and instead of paying Berney $50,000 we decided to go with a public defender. Very bad mistake, we found out later.

Donnie was found guilty of second-degree murder and Lyn was found guilty of child abuse, and was released in three months. Donnie was going to prison for the next twelve years! We were all shocked, to say the least, and my crying time continued. Until you are involved in the judicial system you have no idea how it works, and I would be on both sides of our law system very soon.

Chapter 11

I felt so terribly lost. There was no way I could wrap my brain or my heart around the face that my son was found guilty of murder of a beautiful little baby girl! I was just floating. Marie, my beautiful daughter, was too. She was not doing very well in school. In the past, Donnie had attended Marie's school, and the teacher's were aware that Marie was related to Donnie "the baby killer." Therapy wasn't helping so it was time for a change. Marie would go into an alternative school system until she felt better, or at least could get a handle on the horrible stress she was under. At least she was still going to school

I began attending support groups and became a part of the HIV group that was called WABA, Women

Affected By AIDS. I was also still going to therapy for my back injury, driving Marie back and forth to school, and spending all the rest of my time at the pottery shop, which was my real therapy. I have no idea how I would have made it without Jack and Gayle and their shop. It was the only thing that took me out of my own pity-party. So in a sense, this was actually my silver lining, and it would really come to the forefront later on in my life, and get my life back on track, and Marie's, too. In the meantime, my car broke down, and I was having a really hard time paying my rent. My landlords lowered my rent to four hundred dollars, but I was still having a hard time living on eight hundred dollars. So I could afford no insurance or repairs on my car, no cable TV, no shopping for clothes. Marie was really good about going without new things, so when she did ask for something, it was important to me to get it for her. I was quite guilt-ridden. So my bills were sometimes falling late and I ended up paying late fees which I couldn't afford either.

There were several different agencies that helped "the less fortunate", a category in which I now found myself. It was very hard for me to wrap my head around the events in my life since everything I had ever known was falling apart. I had no way of knowing what to do, and I couldn't tell you if this was ego, pride, or ignorance. Maybe it was just part of being a victim, and I really felt comfortable in that role, 'oh poor little Susie, can you believe what has happened to her?' Nothing was my fault, and I was going to let the whole world know that.

I wasn't getting any more suspicious phone calls. I hadn't seen Joe in my neighborhood for a while, and I was feeling less anxious until the prosecutor, Jay Sweets, called and set up an appointment for me to come into his office. I was so sick from all the medications I'd been prescribed that I couldn't tell you whether I was throwing up from the meds or just plain nerves, and I looked awful. I quit wearing makeup—what was the point? I was crying all the time, throwing up every day. Just getting up every day was traumatic enough, and now I was having all of these appointments all the time. Getting Marie to school was next to impossible, as was getting to my therapy which they had me doing every day now. Additionally I had appointments for agencies to help pay my power bills, telephone bills, electricity bills, food banks, Spokane Aids Network, doctors' appointments—I just wanted to crawl under the covers and die. I was starting to give up on everything. My life was a mess, and I did what I did best, blamed everything on Joe, and cried and cried.

Gayle came over to take me to my appointment with Jay Sweets and helped me to get ready for it. She also was my angel and reminded me that I wasn't going through this just for me, but for all the people who have been knowingly infected with HIV by others.

"Remember all those people you met at the retreat you went to?" She said. "You are doing this for all of them. So get out of your pity-party, and get ready to make a difference!" I felt she had just slapped me into the next world!

I look back on that day in March of 1994 because it was the day my life switched from being a victim to being a survivor. That was a major difference because now I had a purpose in my life. I wasn't fighting for just my life but for that of many others. This was the day I began to see a little light behind that big old black cloud, as well as a full circle from victim to survivor. With my best friend by my side, taking my hand, Gayle told me she was proud of me and would be with me all the way.

"Come what may, Susie, I'll be right here by your side like glue on glue!"

We entered the Prosecuting Office together, and there was my friend, Detective Jimmy Jansen. After introducing Gayle, it was concluded that she would be allowed to remain with me for what would become a life-changing day for all of us, including Joe.

KABOOM! Your boyfriend, Joe, is a predator, and you are not the only woman we believe he has infected! KABOOM! He didn't have HIV when he was in the hospital, as he told you—he had full-blown AIDS!

It was a good thing the wastepaper basket was close because I started throwing up, while the bombshells just kept on coming.

"I am going to charge him with first degree murder, for knowingly infecting you and possibly others. You, Ms. Wyatt, will be the one bringing this precedent case for Washington State. What this means is, this has never been done in a court of law in this state, but we feel that with the investigation Detective Jensen has carried out, there is sufficient evidence in these charges to go forward. Are you okay?"

I must have fainted, because I woke up on the floor in Gayle's arms, with her giving me some sips of water.

About fifteen minutes later, after clearing the fear from my head, and recuperating from what felt like a sucker-punch to my stomach, I said, "Does this mean that you believe me and you are going to arrest Joe?" The answer was yes, that was exactly what they were going to do!

"And you, Susie, are going to be our star witness." OOOKKKAAAYYY, I think.

Jay Sweets and Detective Jansen told me that once the papers had been filed, and Joe was arrested, the media would want to interview me and my life would become an absolute zoo for a while.

"This will not only be a huge case for Washington State, Susie, but only a handful of other states have even tried, with limited success. But know this, I believe you, and the evidence supports this, and this man, this predator, Joe, has got to be stopped from spreading this deadly disease to other unsuspecting people. We will prove this, and we will give you as much protection as you want."

"What do you mean, protection? Won't he be in jail? OH NO! What have I opened up?" I said this with much tribulation. After going through my son's criminal trial and unjust outcome, I wasn't feeling too safe as far as the possibility of Joe getting out on bail and killing me! And that thought was backed up when Detective Jansen was walking us out of Jay Sweets' office. He put his arm around me and asked, "So you still have your gun? Good, keep it close. I will keep you posted on his whereabouts, but until we arrest him, you might want to stay someplace else. He could get wind that we are looking for him, okay? You still have my home number?"

It was really difficult not to go into "the victim mode" as I started to call it. It helped me stay somewhat focused in knowing I had a lot of people on my side. Through this whole ordeal I had the Spokane AIDS network, the WABA group, the Health Department, my family, and most of my friends all standing with me.

I was replacing the brain-washing from Joe, which controlled me into fear and aloneness to a new mantra that empowered me to be a survivor, and it came from my friend Gayle. "Remember Susie, being a victim limits you in fear, being a survivor gives you the strength to change the world. 18 years later I remember it like it was yesterday!

Joe was arrested without incident as they call it, and was sitting in jail awaiting his bail hearing, for which Jay Sweets wanted me to be present in case he needed me to testify. And to my surprise, Richard Lasiter, Joe's ex-parole officer was there. Although Joe was no longer on parole, Richard was there, he said, for me.

Ever since I had met this man and his wife Rose, they have become a permanent heart-link in my life. And when I saw Richard standing there, he hugged me and said, "I wanted to be by your side when you see this predator and watch him being charged, and taken off the streets! You have done a good thing, Sue, and I am very proud of you for doing it!" Wow, and then I melted into his arms and did what I did best; yep, you got it, I cried. And when Joe saw me in court with his cold eyes full of rage and anger, I knew I was dead meat!!!!

Chapter 12

My case manager, Lorie, at SAN (Spokane Aids Network) was put in charge of my health. This was a network that took care of you and helped find you the best medical care in town. They were funded by the Ryan White Foundation. Ryan White was a young man who ultimately died of AIDS, but had gone around the country educating adults and children the truth about AIDS and the prejudices surrounding it. The stigma concerning this disease was horrible no matter how a person had contracted it. Ryan White was just a young boy when he contracted HIV through a tainted blood supply. He was a hemophiliac and needed frequent blood transfusions. But it didn't matter to the public how he got it, he had IT! Things had gotten to the point that the school didn't even want him there in class with the so-called "normal" kids because the AIDS virus might jump off him and infect others! Really, it was that bad! And back in the early 90's that how people thought, Maybe some even today.

So when Lorie from SAN, came over one day for a house visit, she brought with her lots of help. A housing development was going up in the valley (that's what we called Spokane Valley, back then. It's now its own city) for HUD (Human and Urban Development) and I qualified for that. I just needed to apply for it. It would take care of my rent problem, and I could move into a place just for people with HIV. Okay, that sounded pretty good. Then Lorie asked me, "Susie, have you by any chance seen the morning paper today?" I said, "a no why?" That's how I heard about the charges and arrest of Joe, that morning, and on the front page, no less, and that a woman by the name on Susan Wyatt, was bringing these charges. Kaboom!

Within hours of the morning paper being out, Jay Sweets' office had been contacted for statements "for the record," which was the media, and Jay called to ask if I would be willing to do an interview for the paper. The next day a reporter for the newspaper, and a cameraman, were in my living room, and for the first time in my life I was going public to the whole world that I, Susan Wyatt, had HIV and giving out the details of how I had contracted it.

I wanted people to know that ANYONE could get this terrible disease. Little boys like Ryan White, and even "soccer moms", were at risk.

The reporter asked me, "Well, when did you find out that Joe had HIV?" And that would become the million dollar question along with my answer, "I had been told by Joe while he was in the hospital around September twentieth that they, "they" being the doctors, had just diagnosed him with HIV. Yes, we were having unprotected sex." Having to answer this question was so embarrassing. Little did I know that it would become so much worse than just embarrassment. I was putting my whole life on the line, and Marie's life, too. From the time I had met Joe that night when I was in the bar playing darts with my son, until he was hospitalized with some form of pneumonia, had been around two months and, "Yes, there are probably other women that don't even know they are or were infected by him."

Had I not over heard his mother tell Joe's sister's that he had known for years that he was infected, had I left Joe when I found out in Sepember of 92, well lets just say none of this would have happened. I would be on a completely different path in my life, and I would not have been the one to give a voice to so many, and held the infectious spread of this disease, accountable! Little did I know, this would define my life for years to come.

Again I did what I do best—I broke down in tears. Looking back now, I think that the reason behind some of this "crying time" was sheer embarrassment, fear, and guilt. Now it was going to be on the news and in the newspaper. I would become the spokesperson for "victims with a cause," and I could hold up my head and make the best of a worse situation. AH-HA! A silver lining has shown up. Okay, I can do this. That is if I don't get my head shot off. I now had an important purpose in life—I would educate people of all ages about HIV/AIDS and hopefully help to change law in the process. Infected people who knowingly infected other people were finally going to be held responsible for giving them a KILLER DISEASE!!! And my case was charging Joe with premeditated murder, a life sentence.

With pictures taken and my story told, the reporter and photographer left my beautiful little home, and I called Jay Sweets to let him know I had told my story to the media. He let me know that my address would not be used in print nor would my real full name, for privacy. I didn't see where that was very important, but, Oh Baby, I sure am glad someone like him was fully aware that this case would put anyone involved in it, in the limelight.

About ten days after my story broke in the newspapers, on the radio, and TV, I received a letter in the mail from Labor and Industries. To make a long letter shorter, they informed me that, "Because of your post, medical health condition, we will no longer be responsible for your injury or therapy." And, it continued, "You will no longer be getting payments from us, effective immediately." KABOOM! Wow, did that come out of left field. I did not see that coming at all and had no idea what to do. My funds were being cut off, and there was no way I could go back to work. My back injury was still a major health factor in my life, and now I had no therapy, either? Oh no! Now what?

I contacted my civil attorneys, the ones who originally directed me to Detective Jansen and the criminal case. Jim Dominica carefully looked over my notice and said that Labor and Industries might possibly have a case because no one knows how having HIV does or will affect healing of a prior injury.

At this point I was feeling totally overloaded by doctor visits, going to support groups, receiving therapy, taking Marie back and forth to school, and sick of the medications. After the meeting with my attorneys, I went home and crawled into bed and cried!!! I would have liked to have stayed in this state forever, but life does go on, and after a short time I came out of my cocoon and went to pick up Marie from school.

When we got home I sat Marie down and told her what I'd just learned concerning the L&I payments. And that I had no idea what to do except file for help from the state, welfare, where I would at least get medical coverage and food stamps. "And I think, maybe some monies for rent, too," I had said, trying to sound hopeful.

At this point I couldn't tell you why I was so sick. I don't know if it was the overwhelming stress of my life being chipped away with a pickax into nothingness or knowing there was a killer disease swimming around in my body doing as much damage as it could with its sole purpose being to kill me! WHY WASN'T GOD ANSWERING MY PRAYERS! AND WHERE WAS THE SILVER LINING!

The next day Gayle took me down to the Department of Human Services, and I filled out applications for help from the state. An appointment in a few days was scheduled and I showed up a few minutes ahead of time. It took about two hours of waiting before I was called in to go over the papers I had filed. So here I was sitting in this waiting room filled to overflowing with about 75 adults and children in it. I'd begun to feel a little uncomfortable when a stranger came over to a vacant seat next to me, sat down, and said, "Um, excuse me, but are you the lady that was in the paper a couple of weeks ago, ya know, with AIDS?"

How dare this dirty, smelly woman say I had AIDS? Yep that is exactly what was going through my mind. Talk about "pride goth before a fall!"

I responded with a very uppity remark, "If you are going to ask me something like that, shouldn't you at least get the facts right?"

She immediately jumped up and said loud enough for all in that waiting room to hear, "You are her! That woman in the newspaper, the one with AIDS!"

You could hear a pin drop in that room, as people around me quickly got up to move away from me. I was not only petrified with fear and embarrassment, but I could feel all the color drain from my face. Then, mercifully, over the loudspeaker I heard the magical numbers, "Number 162 to door 2." I'm not sure how I even made it to the door, but I do remember collapsing into a chair in a very tiny room and bursting into tears. A lovely and compassionate woman came into the room with tissues and a cup of water and said "We will start whenever you are ready. I know a little how it may feel to be here asking for help, but I am here to help you if I can." I wanted to say that I AM NOT LIKE ALL THOSE LAZY AND DIRTY PEOPLE OUT THERE, I'M DIFFERENT. But thank goodness, that isn't what came out. After a few minutes went by, I was able to compose myself enough to let this lady know what just happened out in the waiting room, and that I am that person, but I don't have AIDS—I have HIV. At least, I thought, it sounded a little better and maybe this kind lady wouldn't bolt for the door! WHEE! She didn't. She even patted my hand and said it was okay, "I have a friend whose son is gay and has AIDS."

"I'm not gay and I have HIV!" I said quietly, with my head hung low.

"Honey, it doesn't matter to me how you got it. I read your article in the newspaper, and I hope you nail that son-of-a-bitch! So let's get down to business and see how we can help."

Wow, okay! I quickly snapped out of my pity-party and we got down to business. About an hour had gone by when she finished and said she would be back in a few minutes after she copied all of my paperwork. She would then let me know how much the grant would be to help me financially and also to cover medical and food stamps. I was definitely feeling better than when I first came in. At least I would get some help. It was only a few minutes later and this lovely lady came back with news that yes, I qualified for financial help and what the amount would be. I looked up at this woman and with alligator tears ready to burst forward said, "Thank you but this won't cover my rent." As she sat down, she took my hand in both of hers and said, "I know, Susan, you will have to find a place to move to. But you do qualify for special housing because of your medical condition and you still have a child at home."

Chapter 13

While driving home from my appointment, I kept mulling around in my brain what to do. I knew I qualified for special housing because my case manager, Lorie, from Spokane Aids Network, had already told me that I did. So I'm thinking that when I get home I'll call her and see how everything is going as far as that housing apartment complex that is being built. Maybe I can move into something like that. Mick, my brother is moving out this weekend, and will be heading back to work on Monday, so I need to come up with something very soon, but what do I do in the meantime about all the other bills?

While driving home, I was approaching Washington Water Power, and ended up pulling into the parking lot, meanwhile trying to gather up the courage to go into the office and tell them I won't be able to pay my bill, and the reason that I couldn't—hoping that maybe they could help me.

I am escorted to a desk and chair when a woman comes over, introduces herself to me, and we sit down.

"How may I help you, Ms. Wyatt?" Well, you know, I began crying. Through my tears I told her, "This is why I wouldn't be able to pay my bill because I had to file for welfare (I was so embarrassed), and this is what they are going to give me as far as money. I don't know what to do but come in here and let you know what is going on. Are there any programs that can help me, you know, till I am able to move into something cheaper?" I remembered she'd said that there were several programs to help people who find themselves in "difficulty." She told me she would be right back with what they had.

Oh, yeah, I thought to myself, I have definitely found myself in "difficulty", as she had put it. What a nice and soft way of saying "You have totally screwed up your life, and don't forget you are doing this to your daughter, too!" By the time the lady came back, I was in the throes of a full-fledged breakdown of tears. The dam had burst, and I just couldn't stop. Finally about fifteen minutes later I was able to calm down. By now several people were clustered around me, bringing me tissues and water, and telling me that things would be okay, they found me some help with my bill for several months, and that would help until I found a cheaper place to live.

Geez—looking back, I feel sooo sorry for those people. What do you do with a hysterical woman? You hope that she calms down really soon before you have to call 911 and transport her to the nearest hospital for evaluation. Thank goodness I did calm down on my own. A kind-faced man in uniform and obviously a security guard stood near me and said, "Ms. Wyatt, we are aware of your story that was in the newspaper. All of us are here with you at this moment, and, I can speak for all of us. How very sorry we are for you and your family. It's no wonder that you find yourself breaking down and crying; I'm sure we would be doing the same thing also. So don't worry your little self, everything will be okay." I remember looking up at his face and seeing such conviction and kindness. How could I doubt him? But, boy oh boy, that silver lining better show up soon, before someone does commit me!

At least when I am driving, I have to concentrate on that, and things I need to do to just have to wait. I had several calls to make when I got home. When I got Lorie, from SAN on the phone, she told me that she had been trying to get in touch with me all morning. "You have been approved for an apartment. That new one I told you about in the valley and if you get in touch with Tony, the guy who is the manager, he can show it to you and let you know when you can move in. They are still finishing up on a few apartments. Can you do that today?"

Well, I jumped on this. Wow, what perfect timing. Ah-ha! A silver lining! And boy, did I need one right in the nick of time! A few hours later I had arranged for an apartment that Marie and I could move into in a month. Just as things were looking up, I get a phone call that Joe had made bail and was out! Oh NO!!!

As I am running over to the Pottery shop, Jack and Gayle's place, I am wondering if he is lurking in my neighborhood and watching me. God, I am so scared, what am I going to do the next thirty days of my life. This fear is controlling me. Then the light bulb goes off in my head. Everything Joe had programmed me to believe, all the fear of being rejected by family and friends, all the times he threatened to kill me if I told ANYBODY—none of these things had come true. And actually the only thing he was right about was Labor and Industries dropping me as a client, which looking back, they did have a point. After all these fearful and scary things Joe had convinced me would happen, the tide had turned. I was the one Joe should be afraid of and I was acquiring the support of people in high places who are going to protect me and who believed in me. So by the time I reached the shop, I had found my conviction! My power! My silver lining! And I am sure Gayle was waiting for this "poor tear-stained face of mine" to burst through the door. But instead I came through those doors with a smile on my face, and hugged my best friend and said, " Millie (her nick-name), I have found my silver lining, my strength !" This time when we collapsed into each other's arms and cried, the tears were strictly of happiness, and they even felt better. "I knew you could do it, Susie, I just knew it!" It's just amazing how when you cry 'happy tears' they feel so much better!

Chapter 14

It was bittersweet, moving into my new apartment. I was coming from a beautiful little home with hardwood floors, built-in book cases on both sides of the fireplace, large-paned glass windows, and a yard that looked as if it belonged in a park. There were more than fifty trees of all different varieties all around the house. In the autumn the variety of colors was absolutely breathtaking, as our Indian summers in Spokane are a must-see, a reward for all of us to enjoy before the cold weather comes.

The apartment that Marie and I were moving into was a real switch compared to what we were used to living in. In the past we'd always had either houses or duplexes, and boy oh boy! This was really small compared to what we had had, but at least we would be safe here. It was a secured building where you had to use a key to get into the main part, then walk down a hall to your apartment, and then use another key to get into that. Never had we lived in a place where you had an inside hallway to your home. I really couldn't call this a home like the places we had in the past, but at least it was new and I could afford it through the subsidized housing I now had. In other words, it was clean, new, affordable, and safe . . .

Before moving we had two huge yard sales, thanks to the help of a lot of friends and family, plus we offered free clothes and kittens to draw people. With the people I had met at Pastor Sally's church and the people whom I'd met at SAN and the health department, the response was huge. I can't tell you how many people came up to me and had said they were so glad I was standing up for myself and fighting in the courts for the change in law, so "All those sons of bitches are held accountable! You go girl, for all of us!" At least that was the gist of it. This case was not just me charging Joe with knowingly infecting me with a disease for which there was no cure, a horrendously painful illness to die from—this was everyone's case.

It had now become OUR CASE, and just in Spokane alone, there were hundreds of cases! But what about statewide or even nationally? How many were there? What about the worldwide situation? That's where the spread of this ugly disease reaches millions!!!

Even though my move was only about six blocks away from Jack and Gayle and their pottery shop, things were going to be different. Now I would have to drive over, instead taking my coffee cup and walking two houses away. I was really going to miss that.

The pottery shop became my lifeline. Many times I would arrive there before Jack or Gayle were even up. They allowed me to come and go as I pleased. Jack had a really awesome stereo system in the shop and we would put on Hootie and the Blowfish, or the Eagles, or a variety of our rock and roll music, and crank it up and just "rock on" in the shop while we all worked on different projects. I could concentrate on applying a variety of decorated lines, designs, and marks on wet pottery that Jack had thrown the night before. Or I would be glazing, and splattering pots, or just cleaning up the shop. Jack was quite a mess-pot, but on the other hand he was an expert potter, and threw some very beautiful things. Jack was also a night-owl. There were times I would come into the shop first thing in the morning, and it would be full of pottery that Jack had thrown until sometimes 5 to 6 AM. Yep, he was definitely a night person. So, thankfully, there was always something for me to do. And for me, it was the best depression pill there was, because I surely didn't need another pill to add to my medication list!

Yes, there were benefits to moving into this apartment, but there were also some drawbacks, and not being as close to the shop as I had been before, for Marie and me it was to be a really big negative. It was also a time for me to stand on my own two feet, and start to figure out some things myself. Like, why? Why was this now my life. What was all of this, my life up to this point, going to teach me? What was this going to teach and share with others? The answers are, still to this day, coming to me. A never ending journey . . .

Chapter 15

It took only a few days for me to realize that most of the residents in this new apartment were gay. And that was because most of the people who were infected, that we knew of at the time, were gay, but there were also a couple of people who contracted HIV, through tainted blood transfusions, and others through "shooting up drugs" with dirty needles. Marie and I were the only mother and daughter there. And you know what? The situation was pretty darned good. They, the "gay guys," were a hoot! We would be front and center when they would dress up "in drag," and they would look better than Marie or me on a good night! They were such good sports, too, but boy oh boy, when some of them were having a "tiff" the DRAMA was on. After a few days the whole thing would blow over and all was well—that is until the next spat, and you only had to wait a few days for that.

Marie and I were the token "straight family" there, and the guys loved to dress us up. It was like we were the fashion models and they were the designers. Some of them would do fashion, some makeup, and others would style the hair. It didn't matter that my daughter and I really weren't going out on a date (my dating ended with Joe); it was just fun, and there were precious few days of that for any of us. So for all my wonderful and special brothers and sisters (you know who you are), I say thank you for the good times, thank you for a safe shoulder to cry on, but most of all thank you for your understanding and encouragement. This was such an unexpected silver lining in our lives, and to think—I almost missed it!!!

I must say that most of the people that lived there were just trying to live a life of some kind of normality, but there seemed to be very little of that. The medications we were all on in one fashion or another made us very ill, and we were all taking many different kinds and different combinations of medications. Back then they called it "a cocktail." Well, I was under the impression that a cocktail was supposed to be good, like a fancy drink or a delicious shrimp cocktail. You know, something you would look forward to enjoying. Well! These cocktails weren't! The pills were usually huge, and sometimes you had to take them on an empty stomach, sometimes a full one; you had to take them every three or four hours. Often you even had to set your alarm and get up in the middle of the night to take your medications. And even when you are throwing all of this up, in a couple of hours you will have to eat some food and take another handful of medications and hope to God you can keep everything down! You were usually taking more side-effect medications than the ones that were supposed to be fighting the virus

It was during this time that I was called to give a deposition for the state's case against Joe. His attorney would be there asking me questions about the charges I and the State of Washington had filed. Joe was not allowed to be present because I still had a restraining order against him. And for the first time since this whole thing started, I felt a sense of strength and truth on my side and a purpose for a whole lot of people who were counting on this trial to go forward and change state law. For the first time since my mom died in March of

1992, I felt her presence. Not just a yellow rose bush in my back yard, but a real rush, and the weight of my mom. And I walked into the prosecuting attorney's office with my head held high, and best of all, NO TEARS!

My rock, Gayle, was with me but had to wait in the waiting room until I came back. As I waited for an officer to come and escort me to Jay Sweets' office, she had reminded me of the mantra she had taught me and it was so profound that I never have forgotten it. "Remember Susie, being a victim limits you in fear; being a survivor gives you strength to change the world. So go change the world!" And with a hug and a kiss on the cheek, she sent me on with the officer, and I swear to God! I really thought I had just been in the presence of my mom. AHH, that sure felt good. But then out of the blue, Kaaabooom!

Chapter 16

Walking into Jay Sweets office I sensed a palpable tension that you could cut with a knife, and I felt that knife was pointed right at my heart as I was introduced to Joe's attorney, William Douglas.

"And you will address me as Mr. Douglas, is that clear?" he said as I shook his hand. And I thought to myself as I was stuffing my fear down to my feet and hoped it stayed there, "You arrogant son-of-a-bitch."

"And you will address my client as Ms. Wyatt, is that clear?" Jay Sweets responded with a strength in his voice that I had never heard before!

Unlike my prosecutor's overall persona, which was tall, on the thin side, always dressed in a wrinkled suit, and usually in need of a haircut, Mr. Douglas was just the opposite. He was about 5'10", well built, about fifty years of age, and dressed as if he had just stepped out on an Armani men's clothing store. In other words, he looked pretty damn good!!!

Mr. Douglas had a rather deep and confrontational voice which was very intimidating to me. When Jay Sweets told me the week prior to this meeting about Joe's attorney and what he was like in court, I chalked it up as courtroom bravado, but Jay's warning turned out to be exactly what he was like. His plan was to intimidate me. Then I remember what Gayle had just said to me, "Being a victim limits you by fear. Being a survivor gives you the strength to change the world."

His first question to me accompanied by his loud and dismissive attitude was, "Ms. Wyatt. when you first had sex with my client, why didn't you insist he wear a condom?" Wow! Good question. I wondered that myself. Why hadn't I? What was it about Joe that wearing a condom didn't even cross my mind, until after our first sexual encounter?

I really hadn't dated very much until about a year before I met Joe. I'd been introduced to Tim in 1991. He was James' friend, and the son of one of the men who worked in the hospital in the ultrasound area. He was a good-looking guy with blond hair, blue eyes, about six feet tall, and he'd just gotten out of the service. He asked me out and I said yes. Wow, my first date really for at least a few years. I was so busy with raising my kids, working full time, soccer games, track, running my kids back and forth to many different events, where did I have the time to date?

Tim and I dated exclusive for about six months. It soon became obvious that Tim had a drinking problem, and one night while very drunk he'd told me that he had not been faithful in our relationship.He said that when he was drunk he'd have sex with any woman that approached him. "I just couldn't say no, honey."

I broke off our relationship the next day when he came over, and I wasn't too upset with him because he was so nice. I told him that I felt sorry for him and that being an alcoholic was most definitely not going to fit into my life or my daughter's. She was my only child left at home, my other two were grown and gone.

I'd grew up in an abusive alcoholic family and I was most definitely not going to live that kind of life again! I had a hard time understanding the whole concept of addiction, but not the fallout.

When I had met Joe in the bar that first time, it was late at night. When the bar closed and we walked out into the night, he seemed quite sober, and asked me out on a date the following week. That had been several months after my breakup with Tim.

In the days when I was growing up, and even after my divorce the main reason men would wear condoms was so you didn't get pregnant although I had heard of STDs, sexually transmitted diseases. After my third child I'd gotten myself "fixed," so getting pregnant was something I didn't have to worry about. And certainly, I reasoned with myself, I would know if someone was infected, wouldn't I? So even though I didn't date much, didn't sleep around, and was "faithful" to the person I was dating, well, that was good, right?

So when I was asked by Joe's attorney, "Why didn't you insist Joe wear a condom? I answered the only way I could, with what now seems like stupid truth, "I didn't think I needed to. He didn't look like he had a disease."

From the first question to the very last, we both became confrontational, and I stood my ground against this pompous, arrogant lawyer, I was empowered by the truth. I was finally able to find my voice and the last thing I said in front of Attorney William Douglas was, "Joe should have told me from the beginning of our relationship that he had AIDS, or at least protect me, and he didn't do anything!!!! He gave me a deadly disease, lied about it in the hospital, acted like he had just found out he had HIV, but in reality he had full-blown AIDS! Mr. Douglas, your client is guilty of murder! A murder he could have prevented! See you in court. This deposition is over!"

At that moment, I didn't know who I thought I was, but I had simply had enough. Two hours was plenty of time to drill me, belittle me, and yell at me as Mr. Douglas had. Jay Sweets was a little taken aback too, and ended the deposition. I had found my strength to change the world; well, at least my life, and I was no longer a victim.

When Joe's attorney left, I looked at the prosecuting attorney and wondered why—why he had let this man talk to me as he had—really angry and mean, and I was pissed at him for that.

He said, "Susie, I allowed him to do that because I needed to see how strong you would be in court and up on the stand, and trust me," he said with a chuckle in his voice, "You will do just fine. I didn't think you had it in you, but I was wrong. Tell me, what changed?" I just looked at him and said, "My attitude. I stopped feeling sorry for "poor little Susie" and started feeling for all the other people I had met who had been infected by someone else who knew they had HIV/AIDS. I spoke from conviction—for all of us."

When I finally made it to the waiting room, Gayle looked up at me, and with a very surprised look on her face when she realized that mine wasn't tear-stained. We both were smiling, and fell into each other's arms, and I said, "Millie, let's blow this joint! I'm starving!"

Chapter 17

My first pre-trial date was in June of '94', and this was mostly about evidence both sides wanted to bring into court. From the prosecuting side it looked like this:

#1—Documentation from Dr. Ruark, of my medical chart and care. This was when I was taking the HIV tests, my health also just before that on my injury from the hospital, and when he passed me over to an Infectious Disease Doctor. What I didn't realize was that he routinely kept meticulous notes not just on me but all his patients.

#2-The CDC (Centers for Disease Control) from Atlanta had also gone over my doctor's medical chart,

---

and that's how they were able to say with confidence exactly when I became infected with HIV—in early September of 1992. Wow!

#3-Depositions from two nurses who were on duty the day Joe told me he had just been told he had HIV. They were going to testify as to how I reacted to this news when I was in the little sitting room just down the hall from Joe's room. I really hadn't even remembered that until it was just brought up in pre-trial. Guess that was some more of the stuff Detective Jansen discovered.

#4-Dr. Susan Cophner, my doctor now. This had to do with her medical field of working with people with HIV/AIDS. I had to remember that this was a fairly new disease, and had only recently come to the attention of the CDC in the 1980s under the assumption that this was a "Gay" disease, because they were being able to track it somewhat in the gay communities and the accompanying behavior patterns. And it wouldn't even be looked at differently until the mid to late 1980s when they began to see the spread into the "straight community"—i.e., women, prostitutes, or soccer moms, I.V. drug users or I.V. tainted blood supplies and even among Blacks, Indians, Hispanics . . . . well, it was now everywhere. Dr. Cophner was treating a variety of patients with this disease, including me. And now the experts were seeing pregnant women and babies being born with HIV.

Joe's attorney was arguing for more medical testing on Joe, because he had stated, "Your Honor, my client is too incompetent to stand trial because of a diagnosis of dementia that has advanced to the state he cannot aid in his behalf."

What? What the hell was this? The Judge granted the defense a continuance for more medical testing on Joe. And seeing him in court that day, he definitely did look pretty bad, so much so that I leaned over to Jay Sweets and said, "Can they do that? He's just faking it!" All the Prosecutor said was, "They are going to try. We will have to wait and see what the medical tests indicate, Susan, he can't fake them. So we will just have to wait and see."

As we stood up to leave the court room, I glanced over at Joe and his attorney, and just for a split second I saw that smirk on Joe's face as he made eye contact with me, and I froze! Oh yes he can, I thought. If anyone can do it, it would be Joe. That was what was programmed into my brain at that split second glance. Why, how can he do that to me? Don't let him see the fear! Don't let him see the doubt. Be strong, be a survivor. Walk out of this room with your head held high.

That was what was playing in my head as we left the court room, and as we swung the courtroom doors open, we were hit with a huge group of media from all over. Not just our state but from around the country! KABOOM!

Chapter 18

Shouts of questions were coming from this group of reporters wanting to know the details concerning this case and the fact the State was charging this man, Joe, with murder—and the "weapon that was used" was HIV/AIDS disease.

Microphones were pushed in my face and questions shouted at me. I did not say a word. I was still playing in my head that smirk on Joe's face, and now this, absolute mayhem in the halls of this court—room area. I wondered how they knew that this pre-trial gathering was even taking place and what was so important that all these people and camera equipment were even there.

Jay Sweets put his arm around me to kind of shield me from the group of reporters, at the same time saying, "We will have a statement for you regarding this case in front of the courthouse in about ten minutes, so please let us pass."

The next thing I remember is that we were in another room down the hall where Detective Jansen had directed us. It was a very nondescript room with only a table with several chairs placed around it. Jay Sweets was very concerned about how much media was present in the hall way of the courtroom, and telling Detective Jansen that they had to make sure that this didn't happen again.

"I felt as if we were walking into an ambush!" He said. "And I don't want that to happen again. And I want police protection around Susan, in or out of this area. That will also be when we are meeting with media. But after today, that will be in a more secured area. Make that happen, okay, Jimmy?"

Sitting across from me at the table, Mr. Sweets told me that when we meet with the media, some of the questions would be directed at me and asked whether I would feel confident in being on camera and answering their questions. I said, yes, I did and if I was unsure about a question I just wouldn't answer it. I remember Jay laughing and saying "Okay, that will be my cue to step in—is that what you are saying?"

"Yeah, that's it, is that okay?"

With a shake of his head we headed out to the front lawn of the Spokane courthouse, greeted with blue sky and sunshine and a mass of media, and my friend Gayle beside me.

"Mr. Sweets, what is it about this case that convinced you to bring a charge of murder against this man?" Someone asked.

I remember his answer so clearly, when he responded with conviction, "The truth. We have done an extensive investigation, as you can imagine, and everything that Ms. Wyatt has told us has panned out to be truthful and provable." Wow! He really believes me. That's all I needed to hear. Mr. Sweets has my life in his hand, and for the first time sense I met him, I felt safe and validated.

"Ms. Wyatt, how are you feeling, and how does your family feel about you having Aids?"

The media ask such stupid questions. Even back then they did. You want to say, "How the hell do you think I feel?" But you don't because the last thing you want to do is piss them off. So I answer their questions. "I am pretty sick with the medications I am on, and the stress of this case. My family supports me and by the way, I don't have AIDS, I have HIV." For some reason that was always important for me to make clear. Like if I was still just HIV infected then I was still one step from AIDS, and still had time to live, because after all, I had a lot still to do.

After about ten minutes of questions, we left and went with Detective Jansen. Jay Sweets had said that as soon as he found the results of the medical tests they were going to run on Joe, he would call me. Then I asked the million dollar question, "So, what happens if he is found incompetent to stand trial, what does that mean?" Remembering Joe's smirk and Jay Sweets telling me that these tests they were ordering on Joe cannot be faked. And?

Chapter 19

"It means that the tests they will be running on Joe are going to determine whether he can aid in his own defense, or that he is so medically challenged from dementia of the brain and cannot aid in his defense." What?

"You mean if the tests find him incompetent, he goes free????" I had said with a huge lump in my throat, tears coming to the surface of my eyes, and hanging onto Gayle's hand for dear life.

"Yes, in a way." And that's the last thing I remember, as I slowly sank to the ground. When I came to, I was still lying there on the ground, my head in Gayle's lap with her holding a bottle of water to my mouth. My face was ashen white and I began crying. A few minutes later as I started to get up, with my best friend's help, I looked up at the prosecuting attorney's face and said, "Please, don't let him get away with this. I'm not the only one he has infected, and who knows who will be next." How he understood those words through my crying in an almost hysterical state, I don't know. But he took my hand and looked into my tear-stained face and said, "Susan, I promise you, he will not walk free!" I could see the anger in his face and feel it in his voice.

It was a good thing Gayle was driving. I felt like I had just been run over by a Mack truck. The medications I was on didn't help either. My doctor had discovered the dosage of one of my meds, AZT, was way too much and corrected "the mistake" and put me on a synthetic marijuana pill called Marinol. It was supposed to help reduce the nausea and give me an appetite. I had lost far too much weight, around thirty pounds in the last three months—weight I couldn't afford to lose. As Dr. Cophner had said, "When you have HIV/AIDS, your weight is something you need, because when you become sick from the virus, it eats up your fat reserve and you could end up with what we call the "wasting syndrome."

Gayle took me home. I knew Marie would be there waiting for me, eager to hear the latest of what happened in court. Oh, I just wanted to go to bed, crawl under the covers and pretend this was just all a bad, bad dream! Walking up to the building, I noticed a man I had just met a few days prior, and introduced him to Gayle. George was a very attractive and had a really fun laugh. When he saw me he waved, and when we got closer, he looked at me and said, "Girl, what happened to you? Ah, come here, you need a hug." And as I introduced George to Gayle, I told him we had just come from court. "Oh okay, I have just what you need. Follow me, you two." George lived only two doors down from me, and when we got to his apartment, he already had tea made. He gave me a joint of real pot, which I smoked and in just a few minutes I felt so much better. The tea was great and George had a way about him that was just fun.

Soon after that we all left and went to my apartment to tell Marie about the day. Having George in hand and my best friend next to me, and me being stoned, at least I wasn't crying, which was a big surprise to Marie. Her boyfriend, Bob, was there. He had been quite a shoulder to lean on for Marie, and they seemed to be committed to each other. But did I know, I was in my own little pity-party world. Marie was very angry about what had happened in court and what that might mean as far as our safety.

"I don't know, honey, we just have to wait and see," I said with more confidence than I really felt. Man, that pot really helped, I kept thinking, even feeling a little in control. That was definitely a new feeling for me. I had smoked pot in the past, not very much, but it seemed to be really different this time. I was going to ask my doctor about this. I felt as though I wanted to go to the pottery shop now instead of to bed, and that's exactly what I did. All of us were going, and we all piled into Gayle's van—me, Marie, Bob, and George, who we promptly named Georgie.

Considering how the day started out, it ended great! There was lots of laughter and playing around in the pottery shop, and a fantastic meal that Gayle and I fixed. It was the first time in months that I could eat a full meal without losing it shortly afterwards in the bathroom, and that was a very good thing.

When Gayle had taken all of us home that night and Marie had left with Bob for a few hours, I sat in my apartment and pondered the events of the day. Slowly I began to see a beautiful silver lining and it was Jack and Gayle, the pottery shop, and the friends that were beginning to come into my life, like Georgie, and soon someone so special that it would change the direction of my life . . . .

Chapter 20

For Marie and myself, living at the apartments was like having all these adopted brothers in our lives. Never in my life had I had so many gay people in my life, and I was liking it and so was Marie. She would tell me years later that those were some of her happiest times.

There was a patio area in the back yard as well as an area where we could have a garden if we were so inclined, and several of us were. It became a meeting place in the summer of 1994. I would go down to the patio area in the morning and have coffee. Soon a small group of us began to meet there each morning to play cards and drink our coffee. And I must say that they seemed to wear much better and lovelier jammies than me.

Steven always had the best coffee, Georgie had the best jammies, and Timmy had the best dramas. His family and friends were just crazy, and it was so much more fun to hear about their dramas than our own. At least there was humor in the stories that he told! And he was a really good storyteller. We would laugh and hoot all morning.

Soon some of the guys started coming over to the pottery shop and Gayle was in "seventh heaven." She was a collector of people and so it went that this became a constant in our lives. Jack wasn't too keen in the beginning about having all these "gay guys" in his life as well as in his home all the time. But as the months passed, he had no choice but to get over it. They were in Gayle's life for good. She had such a huge heart for the wounded and the damaged that, just like me, she took all of us under her wing like a mama bird, and cared for all of us.

One morning, out on the patio, Steven and I were talking about our lives, just the two of us, discovering that we had so much in common. Oh, what a soft soul he was. We became such good friends, a friendship that would last for years, and beyond! His partner, Roy, was an absolutely drop-dead, gorgeous man, but a little bit on the crazy side. Later on I discovered that he was bipolar.

Lorie, my case manager from SAN, had come out to see me and a few of the other residents, and said she had some good news for some of us; Steven was one of "the others". There was a retreat coming up the end of August at Coeur D' Alene lake which would be for several days, and if we wanted to go, there was space for us. WOW . . . . That was awesome news! At a lake? I was really excited at the prospect and hoped I would be in better shape to cope than I had been at the first retreat . . . .

Steven had been to this retreat the year before and said that I would really enjoy it.

"Susie, this one is right up your alley; they have crafts, really fun water sports, and lots of time to spend getting to know others from around the Pacific Northwest."

I had shared lots of personal things with Steven, especially how shocked I was when I went to the Strength for the Journey retreat in 1993. But it was now nearly a year later and I had grown up quite a bit in the HIV/AIDS community. I hoped that maybe this one would have a little laughter and humor to it. It would be a real change for me, even if for only for a few days. It would be a great opportunity to meet other women living with this disease, and Linnie was going to be there.

Lynn had become a very good friend, the one who told me of Dr.Cophner and suggested I have her for my doctor, which I did. Also Lynn had been instrumental in getting me involved in the Speakers Board. This was through Spokane Aids Network and the Spokane Health Department. I had been taking different classes to become educated in the facts concerning this disease as well as the proper terminology surrounding it. If I could just find some way to quit crying when I started to talk about what happened to me, then maybe I could get up in front of people and educate them on how I became infected—and maybe, just maybe—it wouldn't happen to them.

I had to wait until after my court case was over. Jay Sweets didn't want me talking about this in a public forum in case I said something that could be challenged in court. I had really no idea why, because everything I would be saying was the truth.

As Jay said, "We want to try this in a court of law, not in the media, Susan. Trust me on this one. This is too big a case to end up losing it because of something that you said that was taken out of context."

Also Roy, Steven's partner, was on the Speakers Board. And it looked like we all were going to go to the retreat! At least this time I would know some of the people attending. Maybe I would find some quiet time during the retreat when I could talk to Roy about this speaker's board. Either way, I was really looking forward to this retreat to be held the end of August of 1994. At least, I wouldn't have my rose-colored glasses on!

Chapter 21

In July of 1994 we were in the middle of a mild summer when court was set to present Joe's medical tests to the court, and I was to be there, front and center, seated right across the table from Joe. I was still very leary and fearful of this man; he could still get to me. All of the old programming was still trying to hold me hostage, but I had a new mantra I was working on: "Being a victim limits you in fear; being a survivor gives you strength to change the world!"

Marie wanted to go to court with me. It was the first time she had even suggested wanting to be involved.

"Honey," I said, "I don't know if that's a good idea. First of all, Joe will be there, and secondly, the media will be there filming all of us and will probably want a statement. Your friends will see you and connect the dots—are you sure about this?"

"Mom, I'm not a baby anymore, and I want to see Joe and show him that I am not afraid of him! I am a survivor too, mom!"

You know, she was right. My little girl was not a baby any more, and if you are a parent, I'm sure you can picture the scene—a 16-year-old teenager standing in front of you, arms crossed, letting you know in a strong voice, telling you for the first time that she is a whole lot stronger that you were able to even wrap your brain around. Wow! I was totally not expecting this but I remember it so clearly. This was the moment when my little girl became a young woman, and boy, oh boy, she sure seemed a lot stronger than me.

Then she said, "Besides that, mom, Bob and I will be there to protect you." As I started to laugh we all had a three-way hug.

"Mom, you have to wear makeup and a really cool outfit so Joe can't see how he has destroyed your life, okay?" So the morning of this pre-trial motion, there were five gay men in our apartment, doing our makeup, hair, and choosing what we should wear, and I really must say that I think they got a kick out of this. Georgie was the one who had final say on how we looked.

"Don't make them look like drag queens on a runway, just make them look like the beautiful women they are—got it, girls! Keep it simple."

When they were done, both Marie and I looked very beautiful—actually we really looked awesome.

"Whatever you do, don't cry! And if you do, just dab, don't wipe," Georgie said with a hug and a kiss on my cheek. And it was Steven who reminded me that, "Susie, you are representing all of us who don't have a voice, so go get 'em, girl! You can do this! Besides that, you have bodyguards that will be there!" I looked at my very special friend and said, "And you know this how?"

When Marie and I stepped outside to go to court, about thirty people were present, ready to escort us to court. How they did it, I have not a clue, but leave it to a bunch of queens, to know how to organize an "event". We knew most, but not all, of them. And what a mix of beautiful people they were. Lynn was there too. "Susie, when we get to court there will be more people. Hope you don't mind." I hugged Lynn and told her that this was absolutely the best. For the first time I felt that this whole situation was so much bigger than me, and I was now very much up for the challenge of what was just a pre-motion. What was this going to look like by the time we went to trial? However, just as I got comfortable, though, KABOOM!

Chapter 22

We met Jay Sweets and Detective Jimmy Jansen at Jay's office. Neither one of them looked very happy, and I didn't understand why they both looked so gloomy.

"Susan, we have a problem," Jay said with anger in his voice, and I'm thinking, "Oh, God, no, what has Joe done? Did he beat the tests?" My eyes filled with tears and I quickly sat down with Marie, Bob, and Gayle beside me, and we heard that yes, the tests were back, and it looked as though they were going to fight for incompetence.

"What does that mean? What are you saying?" And in my mind I am telling myself "don't cry, don't cry, don't cry, damn it! DON'T CRY!"

"We'll find out soon, but I wanted you to know that there is a chance that Joe will be found to have advanced dementia and cannot aid in his defense. I promise you, Susan, he will not go free, okay?" Jay spoke with such conviction that I almost believed him.

As we were escorted to the third floor of the Spokane Court House and came through the heavy wooden doors there was a mob of reporters who immediately began taking pictures and asking questions that at this point there were no answers to. Immediately before we went through those doors Jay Sweets had told me to not respond to anything the media might throw at me. Well, that was easy for him to say, I thought. And what a mob there was. The hallway was fully crowded. And when Marie and I came through there was a very loud cheer that went up for us and I think it was so powerful it even caught the media off guard. It was our friends, the ones from our apartment building, people I remembered from the Strength for the Journey retreat, and the people from the different organizations I was now part of, and many that I didn't know. It was just like Georgie and Steven had said, "You are our voice!"

Jay bent down and asked me with a whisper in my ear, "Who are all of these people?" I had to laugh a bit and say, "I guess I have more friends than I thought of." Marie was smiling, and through the shouts of, "You go, girl!" and, "We are here and we stand with you." "Wow, mom," Marie had leaned over and said, "this was worth it, don't you think? Now everyone will know! Mom, NO SECRETS!" Well, you know the old saying, out of the mouths of babes!

When we entered the court room it was really full, and I thought, "Who are all of these people?" Then I saw Joe. OH MY GOD! He looked like death warmed over, really! I was shocked. What in the world had happened to him? He had on a blue long-sleeved shirt, and slacks, a cast on one arm, bruises and stitches on his face. That wasn't the shocker, though; it was the fact that he looked like a 90-year-old man—stooped over, emaciated, with a hollowed-out face that looked like he belonged in a zombie movie! Well, he couldn't fake that, could he? What was I afraid of? I looked behind me at Marie as I was being seated at the prosecutor's table, and she had a look of shock on her face too. Then I remembered, this could be me some day . . . .

I didn't understand how someone, who just a few months ago, could look at me and put the fear of God in me with just a wink, look as though he didn't have long to wait "to meet his maker." How could that be? That question was about to be answered.

Chapter 23

The Honorable Judge Carl Boggs entered the court and took the bench, and with a hush in the court room, I swear you really could hear a pin drop. I looked over at Joe and wondered if I was going to end up looking like that. I had seen people with that look at the first retreat I had gone to, and now Joe was wearing the "face of AIDS." It was called the "wasting syndrome," which seemed to be eating at patients from the inside out. And it had only been a few months since I had seen him. Could it happen that fast? I guess so.

It seemed that the tests they had run on Joe did show advanced dementia, a form of Alzheimer's, which left him incapacitated and unable to aid in his own defense. Did this mean that the case had just come to a screeching halt?

The precedent case would go no further in the courts of Washington State, and the case of Wyatt vs. Roberts was over. In the meantime, since he had admitted to infecting me, he would be sent to a criminal hospital to live out his days, and still get the care he would need to treat his disease, but also protect the public from his ability to infect others.

When I looked over at Joe this time, I saw a pathetic, sick man whom at one time I had loved. Not all of the memories were bad, and regardless of the outcome of this case, I saw such sadness in his eyes, and then he mouthed the words, "I'm so sorry, Susie." My heart broke.

We all stood as Joe was taken from the courtroom in handcuffs, and I heard someone in the room crying. Maybe, I thought, that was his mother. I didn't look around. As soon as the Judge left the bench, he invited us, the attorneys and me, into his chambers. I was about to burst into tears when Marie came up to me and said, "Mom, stay strong, don't cry. You'll ruin your makeup"

Marie had said with a little laugh. "I think you have quite a story to tell, and you aren't done, mom. You'll be okay." Looking at this person standing next to me I wondered who this grown-up young lady was in my little girl's body.

As we entered the judge's chambers, I was struck at how normal it looked—as though I had walked into an ordinary person's office, with bookshelves along one wall, a large desk with papers covering the top. Pictures of his family and framed diplomas were displayed on another wall and several chairs, a couch, and a coffee table with lamps shaped like globed street lights tastefully completed the room, which had the smell of fine pipe tobacco.

"I would have liked to seen this go to trial. It was a good case and had merit." He said it with a strong conviction. "Maybe you can make this part of your campaign, Jay, if you choose to run for Director of the Prosecutor's Office. I don't think this is the last we have heard of this happening to others. Have you seen that crowd out there? Who are they?"

Somebody inside of me spoke up. "Your Honor, most of that crowd out there are people who became infected the same way I did, or who know others who were, by someone who knew what they had and didn't care about anyone else they infected, and ended up looking like Joe and dying of this heinous disease that has taken away our whole life. I'm now on welfare, getting food stamps with no hope of ever going back to work. I will die poor and never be able to do things I always hoped I would. I'm sicker than a dog because the medications are trying to kill the virus but are poisoning me at the same time . . . . this has got to stop! And everyone in this room can take note . . . this issue of accountability has just begun!"

Well, I guess I just threw down the gauntlet. We would see what happens; I am ready to face the media out there. I looked up at all these men in the room and said, "Let's go. I have something to say." Certainly Jay Sweets should have known me by now, that when I found my voice, I meant business. It happened when I was giving my deposition to Joe's attorney, and it had just happened again. I got up and walked out of the judge's chambers back into the courtroom where my family and friends were waiting for me with Jay in tow, saying, "Now let me do the talking." Ha! That wasn't happening, I thought. These people had been calling the shots this far, and this is where it was going to end. With me, my daughter, and Gayle arm in arm we burst through the doors of the courtroom ready for the media and cameras. My life would never be the same!

Oh, just in case you are wondering, my makeup looked great . . . . Thanks boys!

Chapter 24

Jay Sweets explained what had just happened in court concerning the precedent case—that it basically wasn't going to set new law, because it was never an issue of who had infected me. Joe had confessed earlier that he had infected me but it was consensual—yeah, right! Jay told the crowd that this case could be used in conjunction with another case in the future to lay foundation for a future case that had merit. "But, I'm sorry, not today," he said to the crowd.

"Ms. Wyatt, how do you feel about this?" one of the reporters asked. I have to say even today, reporters ask the stupidest questions! You want to say something just as stupid back at them, like, "Oh, I feel just wonderful, this is just the happiest day of my life!" Yeah, right!!! So instead of answering their questions, I chose to begin my public speaking career right then and there. Then we would see what they did with it, and how it would come across in the newspaper and the evening news.

"I would first like to say that this just wasn't my case, but thousands of people who have found themselves knowenly infected by someone else, indiscriminate of race, religion, gender, or even age. Until there are laws and harsh penilities to bring to justice ANYONE who spreads this horrible, painful and expensive disease, this will continue! The next time it just may be you, or someone you hold dear to your heart. Anyone who is sexually active! Anyone!"

Marie was asked a question of how she felt about what had happened in court, and how she felt about her mother coming forward and exposing the person who had infected me and how I had become infected, and to this day I remember every single word she said.

"First, I want to say how proud I am of my mom. We are just now learning about HIV/AIDS in school and I hope someday she can go around to schools and tell kids her story, because kids are having sex, too. Most of all I hope my mom doesn't end up looking as bad as Joe does, and we don't have to be afraid anymore."

WOW! I was so proud of her and that is when I started crying. Interview over. By the time we got home, I was totally drained and exhausted and went straight to bed. I woke up the next day, ready to begin my new life.

It was difficult for the rest of the family to understand, but at least Joe would be in a place where he would receive appropriate medical treatment and be safely locked up. In my heart I will never forget how awful he looked, and I prayed that that wouldn't happen to me. This Wasting Syndrome was painful, debilitating, and ugly and I didn't want any part of it—like I was going to have a choice!

I settled quickly into my new life and began going to classes on "Speaking in Public", which was offered through the Spokane Health Department. I was also on the Ryan White Board, an organization of monies allocated to states, counties, and rural areas, for various necessities such as gas vouchers, food vouchers, and help with paying for medications until eligible for some state insurance.

I was also a member of the board for WABA, Women Affected By Aids, one of the most desperately needed support groups available at the time. Why? Because we women were a growing group that was becoming infected and no one was talking about it!

Men were bringing this deadly disease home to their wives—dirty little secrets that no one would discover for years. Women would become pregnant and give birth to children with AIDS before they would even find out. Or their spouse would become very sick with a number of AIDS-related illnesses. This would also take away income the spouse may have had because they are too sick to work. Additionally, employers and other employees didn't want anyone with AIDS in their work force, so as soon as word got around the person would be "let go" for any number of other reasons. Then these families were without income, health insurance, and the stigma of AIDS affecting their children and family, as was the situation in my daughter's case.

Marie was going to be attending an alternative school in the fall. This was her idea, saying, "Mom, my life has changed too, and I don't want to go through all the whispers and looks—you know what I mean." Yes, I knew exactly what she was talking about, and yes, I took the blame for that, too. But despite everything, we still had each other and the pottery shop!

By the end of August I was getting all my things together for the retreat on the Coeur D' Alene Lake in Idaho. It was only about thirty miles from where I lived, and I was truly ready for it. My expectations were so low there was no way I would be let down. My roommate was going to be my friend Lynn, and it was at this retreat that my relationship with this amazing woman went straight of my heart!

Lynn was a twelve-year survivor, and at the time this was a really big deal; and in August of 1994, I was going on my second year and very sick, from the medications. Many of us were either on Marinol, a synthetic form of marijuana that made you either feel like a zombie or wasn't strong enough to handle the pain, or you were, as the doctors said, as self-medicating with marijuana. The latter was the category I fell into as it seemed to be the only thing that made me feel better and I could function. I could eat and keep my meds down and still clean house, go to speaking engagements, meetings, the pottery shop, and just be alive!

Lynn was to become my mentor in all things relating to HIV/AIDS. I learned how to stay alive! I learned how to turn every day into a dream come true, "Because you are alive to tell about it!" And that was her mantra. She helped me find a very important silver lining in my life with HIV. And that was that I'm alive to tell about it! It was also the beginning of Lynn and me doing speaking engagements together, and what an impact it was making!

There were times she was too sick to go and I would do them by myself. I still couldn't get all the way through a speech without crying, and trust me it wasn't something I faked. And at the time, it had quite an impact on the listeners. To most of them I looked like their mom, because I was able to talk to junior high and high school kids. I always had the teachers tell the kids to write out their questions and we would collect them when I finished speaking. I would then answer as many questions as we had time for. That was the silver lining in doing these engagements because that way they wouldn't be embarrassed to ask "real questions", in front of the other kids—like "can you catch HIV from oral sex? Or what's the safest way to have sex?" I got that one a lot. Because I was able to answer their questions honestly and because they felt my pain and tears during my speech, they were brutal in wanting the truth. And from me they got it and I am very thankful that the schools in Spokane were so open to this kind of teaching—to be able to show the younger generation a different face to AIDS, to let all people know "this could happen to you."

I was a very acceptable-appearing person with HIV. I was a white single mom of three kids. The soccer mom, the cookie maker, the mom who always had other peoples' kids staying the night—that was me before. Now I stood in front of people to remind them that I could be their sister, mother, aunt, even grandmother, soccer mom, Sunday school teacher, or even their neighbor. That was the biggest impact of all—me standing up in front of a group of strangers and saying, "Hi, my name is Susie, and I have HIV!"

Chapter 25

I really enjoyed the retreat although it was very different from the Strength for the Journey retreat. There was much more time available to get to know each other, and a craft area where there was a variety of things to make, and we all made tye-dyed shirts. The classes we had our choice to go to were really cool and different. There were dance classes, to legal information about wills and power of attorney, how to deal with the loss of friends and loved ones, to classes on cooking—a very wide variety that was really good, as well as lots of outdoor activities.

One of the most important things I took away from this retreat was the fact that I had a choice of how to live my life; how to become my own advocate in both my health and my private life, as well as how to be able to be pro-active in living. No longer did I stand on the sidelines and let everyone else take care of me. I did my own research on the medications I was taking and no longer did I take a pill just because my doctor said to. I began to question all aspects of my medical care, and that really helped me stay as healthy as I possibly could.

Nevertheless, all kinds of medical issues kept coming up. I would break out in very painful boils mostly in my private areas of my body. They needed be lanced and drained, sometime stitches had to be put in. They were always very painful and would take weeks to clear up. The only thing the medical providers could come up with was that it was probably some kind of AIDS defining/related infection, and they would put me on antibiotics for two weeks and we would wait for the next outbreak. This was to occur throughout my life. And it would also put me in a dangerous situation of becoming immune to anti-biotics because I was on so many of them. It really became a vicious cycle and my health was always an issue as well as the only constant in my life.

In the fall of 1994 I settled into my apartment living, continuing to work at the pottery shop, and doing speaking engagements. One day I received a call from the law office I had originally gone to in 1993, and they wanted me to come in to talk about the case.

The waiting room in their law office was the complete opposite of the one at the prosecuting attorney's office. It was really beautiful, with a fishing theme, and the pictures of awesome areas around eastern Washington where someone was fly fishing. It was a nice, comfortable place to wait, and I didn't have to wait for long.

John Clark and Jim Delmonico talked to me about the criminal case and how sorry they were to not have gotten a precedent conviction in the case.

"Susan, the reason why we called you in today," Jim said, "Is because we don't think this case is over!" KABOOM!

Chapter 26

"We also investigated your claim and found some very interesting things. As you know, Detective Jansen is a friend of ours, and he also found some things that were not a part of the criminal case, but could definitely be a civil case."

Wow, I surely wasn't expecting this. The first thing I told them was that I already had done at least a dozen speaking engagements, so my story was already out there. And I was very surprised when they said that it didn't matter, they thought they had a case against the Department of Corrections, specifically David Bowman, Joe's first corrections officer upon getting out of prison.

"I can't do that," I said. "I've done speaking engagements for them and Richard Lasater, Joe's second parole officer, is a really good friend of mine and so is his wife, Roseanne!"

So they started to lay out their case to me. When they were done, I was shocked! In a nutshell, when I was introduced as Joe's girlfriend to his parole officer, it was understood that my relationship was more than just as a casual acquaintance. Thus I should have been informed, right then and there, of Joe's HIV/AIDS status.

Now you might be asking yourself about confidentiality. That was also brought out in the criminal pre-trial case—how does it work and is everyone protected under the law, to not be discriminated against because of their status of HIV/AIDS—positive?

Back in the 1990s this was very important. People were losing their jobs just because they tested positive, not because they couldn't do their job. This situation could destroy their life as well as others who might even be seen with them. Real education on the subject needed to take place and it needed to be quickly. People still believed that just by being in the same room with an HIV person, the virus could somehow jump off of them and infect you! Seriously, this was the mentality at the time!

I remember being asked over to this woman's house for dinner one night, and she said, "Could you bring over your own silverware and glass? You understand, don't you?" I would have loved to have ripped into this woman just for being so ignorant, but I didn't. I just smiled at her and informed her that, "No, I don't think so, and could you please step back, so I don't catch something from you, like stupidity!"

That's why there were in place such strong confidentiality laws in the late 1980s and early 1990s. Laws which continue to this day. What made grounds for a civil lawsuit was because Joe's case had no confidentiality secured to it. Why? What was the reason?

When Joe was arrested for selling black tar heroin, sometime in the late 1980s or early 1990s, he used the court to gain a sentence downward, on a medical condition, and that medical condition was that he had HIV. That made his disease a matter of public record and rendered his personal health issue public and open to the public, including the Department of Corrections of Washington State. It also so stated that when he was released from prison, his file was what they called "red flagged." And that meant Joe had no protection in his file, and when I was introduced to David Bowman as Joe's girlfriend, I should have been informed right then and there of his HIV status. However, I was not. I was not to know for several months later that "he had just found out," and that was when he was in the hospital with pneumonia.

No one had ever asked me, "Do you know he has had this disease for years?" Never was I asked. Here I was, all ready to get on to carving out a life for myself. Now I was finding out that David Bowman should have informed me when he met me . . . . If he had, I might never have contracted HIV. Oh, goody! I had someone else to blaim!

When the CDC was called in on my criminal case, along with my doctor's records they had obtained, they were able to determine I became infected around the second week of September of 1992. I was introduced to Joe's parole officer, David Bowman, in July of 1992. Aaaah . . . Bombshell!

That is what started the case, Susan Wyatt vs. The Department of Corrections of Washington State and David Bowman. My attorneys were very ready to continue my case in the courts and, "We can bring all of this back into the media, and still be able to strengthen for a precedent case. All these legal things would leave their mark in the courts and others could use the information for their cases if it could help.

"Oh, by the way," I was told, "We have found one of the two other women he may have infected!"

I had forgotten all about them. I was so wrapped up in my own life that I had forgotten about the woman he had been living with before he was arrested—and what about the woman he was with before I met him in that bar, that Thursday night back in 1992? Oh, MY GOD!

How much of this was really going on out there—people infected by people who know that they have a contagious, deadly disease, and are not held accountable for basically destroying someone else's life. What kept going through my mind was that I knew of the woman Joe was with when he was arrested. I knew her name as well as the fact that she had two small children. She might not even be aware that she had been infected and by whom . . . . and could see her passing this disease on to others without even knowing she has HIV? But it wasn't Amber that they had found. Someone else. Char was her name,

That is one thing I personally didn't have to worry about. I wouldn't be giving this silent killer to someone else as it would be very hard to live with the guilt of infecting anyone else. At least I could find comfort in that, but many people I have met and done speaking engagements with didn't have that comfort. From them I heard things like, "That is one thing you can count your blessings for, honey, because it hurts like hell to know I gave this to the one person I loved and had to watch them die!"

I met several people at the retreat who sang the same song of sorrow and regret. One of the classes offered at the retreat was called "Be Kind to Yourself," and it dealt with the issue of guilt and depression. I signed up for this class and so had my friend Steven. They ended up moving it to a larger room because there were so many more attendees than the staff had anticipated.

The class emphasized how to forgive yourself, and this was a real tear-jerker for me. I had to bring up within myself my choices and decisions, and the consequences of those choices. But it was so many others in the class who shared that knowingly they gave HIV to the people in their lives that they love and had loved, that really broke my heart. It also brought out a very unexpected silver lining.

I was given a gift of not only knowing who infected me, but when it happened. There would never have been a trial, criminal or civil, had I not stayed with Joe all those months and overheard that conversation his mother was having with his sisters in the kitchen of his mother's home that Fourth of July weekend back in 1993 . . . "Oh, he has known for years he has HIV" . . . .

It became very important not only for this new case I was involved with, but for Amber Stewart, Joe's girlfriend at the time of his arrest and conviction for selling heroin, that we find her . . . to let her know she needed to be tested to see if she was infected with HIV. And all I could think of was that she had two little children, and if she was infected, how were her kids going to be taken care of. Damn! How many people had Joe really infected? But we needed to focus on finding Amber . . .

Char actually contacted my attorney's, when she had read about my criminal case.She had told them that she had met Joe through some friends of hers, and that she was only with Joe a few times. But after my story was in the paper she went and got tested, and was positive.

Mr. Clark had told me about her and that she didn't know if she had infected others or not. "It took a lot of courage and strength for her to come forward, Susie. She was a broken woman! I let her know that we wouldn't use her in court if at all possible, and if we did, we could protect her identity."

Soon, though, I was to find out that not everyone wanted to know, because as long as they didn't know for sure, they could stick their head in the sand and not be accountable for their actions.

This was now in the hands of the law office of Cray, Clark, and Delmonico, and soon they would be filing charges against the Department of Corrections of Washington State, and David Bowman, Parole Officer.

Chapter 27

Towards the fall of 1995 I had settled in as a more or less permanent fixture of the pottery shop, and I was packing up the little red truck with pottery boxes and setting up tables at farmers' markets and small crafts fairs around the Spokane area as well as Northern Idaho. I would leave early on Friday or Saturday mornings and would be home with monies when the shows were over. It was kind of fun, even though by the time I got back I would be exhausted.

Jack and Gayle always did "the big show", Custer's Arts and Crafts Show, which was huge and held at the fairgrounds in Spokane. This was where they made the bulk of their monies for the year, which hopefully would tide them over until next year. They had to clear at least $20,000 at this show, so we were really cookin' in the shop, getting ready for the big event. Jack started talking about relocating the pottery shop over to the Washington coast, somewhere on the beach.

"If we were to move, we would want you to move with us. Could you?" Both Jack and Gayle asked. So, not all of my bombshells were bad.

Marie thought it was a good idea. "A fresh start for both of us," she said with excitement in her voice. I agreed with her completely. Yes, we could put all of this behind us and live by the ocean, how cool would that be!!

We did really well at the craft show. They met their goal and then some, and we started to look for properties on the coast where we could have a big room for the pottery shop, and living quarters for all of us. I was also borrowing a lot of books from the library on getting my life back on track. Self Help books on how to heal a broken heart, how to find happiness, making good decisions—anything that could help me find a path to healing my life, both health wise and spiritually. I had really damaged my spiritual soul, and I didn't know how much time I had to do this, but I knew there had to be a way to forgive myself and maybe one day even to forgive Joe. As long as I carried this anger and righteous indignation, (also known as pride and ego) around with me, I was never going to grow from this. I didn't want to be the person I was, always pointing the finger at someone else as to why I was in this mess.

It was through the help of my friend, Richard Lasater that was pointing me in the right direction. Richard came over one day to talk about the possibility of me doing speaking engagements for the DOC, not only in their safety education classes but also an "offender's group," that he and John, another officer, were offering. The group they were spearheading had to do with offenders being confronted by their victims telling the story of how their life had changed, and the effects it had had on their entire family. They were also trying to get the courts to make this a mandatory class they, the predator, offender, victimizer—whatever you wanted to call them—had to take.

It was kind of ironic that here I was, on the one hand suing the DOC, and on the other, doing speaking engagements for them. It all had to do with their responsibility to the public to keep us safe, and confidentiality of one's right to privacy. They themselves had to change their policy, and that was only going to happen in a court of law. This is something that many of the DOC officers wanted, because they were the ones who saw first-hand the damage of this with people coming out of prison—who may or may not been infected in prison (most likely they were infected before they went in), and still not being held accountable for infecting others.

They also had to find a way to keep the men and woman who were entering prison with HIV segregated from the rest of the prison population. It was a big and expensive problem for the DOC to figure out, and even a bigger problem once the prisoners were released and on probation.

It was rare to have this come up because not too many people at that time knew they were infected, let alone telling the world in open court, once found guilty of a unrelated crime, that you need the courts to be lenient with your sentence because you have a contagious disease and wouldn't get the medical care or safety that you would need. Can you imagine a fight in prison and then several people or even one person contracting HIV through a fight with blood and cuts on them? If they could prove that it resulted from that fight in prison,(he didn't have it before he or she went in) the state would be held liable. Now testing is done. Once convicted of a crime, prisoners are tested for any and all contagious diseases, including HIV. Back in the 1990s though, this was just starting to be a problem, but in a very short period of time it would become a very BIG problem.

What was happening in this court case was going to help the DOC to change their laws to include informing others who might potentially be in contact with a released parolee of his or her medical condition, including whether this person has a disease that they could contract. It was called "Protection of the Population." It took a few years, but it did work.

When Richard asked me if I would be willing to speak in front of a class of offenders, I always said, yes! I felt that what John and Richard were trying to do was very important, and could maybe save someone's life in the process. I remembered that they took very good care of me and afforded me all the safety and security I needed. I was never left alone with any one of them and Richard was on me like glue. I would answer questions afterwards, but only after they had been checked to make sure there were no threats or profanity in them. As I said, they were extremely protective of me.

In doing these classes with Richard and John, I was starting to hear things like, "What is your responsibility in becoming infected?" or, "If you had it to do over again, what one thing would you change?", or "It seems you have a problem just like us, in making good choices." Bulls-eye!!! Yep.

What was it about me that had caused me to make such horrible choices, which nearly cost me my life? (or were they) Why? I would ponder that question for many years to come. I had to find a way to live with this, all of this. Not just the infection or how I got it, but why. What life lessons was I supposed to learn? What was it that my soul needed to experience, to learn from what? Couldn't I have chosen an easier path to learn from? Well, I guess not. But oh! What amazing answers I was going to find, because I wanted too. I didn't want to just be someone floating through life, defined by

HIV. I wanted to be able to live in my own skin, to be able to shine brightly just like a silver lining or maybe even with some jewels in my crown when it is all said and done with. I want to be able to love me. I want to be someone whose life meant something, someone my children and family could be proud of. I want to be able to say some day, "I love my life," and mean it! I want to live a life of Joy. Is it too late? Or am I just dreaming, wearing rose-colored glasses, as they say. Well, I can try. I have nothing else to lose, or do I?

Chapter 28

Around April of 1996, I found myself totally involved in two things—the speaking engagements around the Pacific Northwest, and the pottery shop. We started to look seriously for a relocation place for the pottery shop, and Jack wanted to be by the ocean, the Pacific Ocean.

The civil case was still plodding along, basically left to the attorney's and the state's attorney general, and I had stopped crying! At least most of the time. I was beginning to get used to having to be on all these meds. Some of them you had to take with food, some on an empty stomach. Some you took an hour before or an hour after eating, some at night, some as soon as you got up, some four times a day, some three times a day, and then you add in the mix of what to do when you throw them up? Talk about making this a little difficult! And the most important thing they, the doctors, were pounding into our heads was the word, ADHERANCE! Well, this was next to impossible, and many of us failed.

I would get so fed up with all these meds, that at times I would just quit them! We called it "our sabbatical." We, and I am speaking for a lot of us, would just quit, and for several weeks or months we felt great, and then the medical tests would come back, and we would be much worse than when we quit. This stealthy invader was doing some pretty heavy damage to our bodies. Time to pay the piper, and when we, I, did this, it was like climbing back up the mountain again. I was starting to break out in the huge boils on a more consistent time line, at least a couple times a month.

I have heard that getting boils means that I am holding anger inside me, and that is how the anger is releasing itself from my body. Okay, so if that's true, why does this show up in all of my siblings? Are we all angry? Or is some of this genetic? My dad had them and all of us kids had some form of them, but not as large or painful as mine. The professionals had no answer for me. They would simply write out another prescription for antibiotics. And said 'it's an AIDS thing. I suffered on . . . .

In June of 1996, Jack, Gayle and myself headed over to the Washington Coast, about 350 miles west, to check on some properties for sale. Wow, was that ever fun! Some of the guys from the apartments were on board to move with us and also help out in the shop, so we needed to find a place to house at least six people as well as Jack and Gayle. And we found it!!!

Copallis Pottery Cove was bought outright. It was an old school building complete with classrooms, bathrooms, kitchen, cafeteria, and gym. Lots of windows and lots of room for all of us to spread out. Perfect!!! And we all were so excited. I finally talked Steven and Roy into moving with us, because Steven had become such a big part of my heart, and this move was going to be such a happy time for all of us. It would be a new beginning. We all wanted that. We had nothing to lose, so why not. Steven had also become very close to Gayle who loved collecting all of us wounded souls, and by the time we started to pack up the shop, it became a reality.

Jack's father died suddenly in July, and we were all very saddened by this. He was a really cool man, always with a smile on his face, and like Gayle, he loved to be around all of us crazy people. He could tell wonderfully funny stories that would last for nearly an hour. Oh, how we loved Jackie! Every Sunday Gayle would fix a big Sunday dinner with at least six guys from the apartment, me, Marie and her boyfriend, Bob, who was now a permanent fixture in our lives, and Jackie. It was so much fun!

Jackie died very suddenly from a massive heart attack, and we all lost a very special friend. We had to stop everything and work on getting his affairs in order. While going through his home, it was like walking through a time capsule, back to when Jack and his sister were growing up. We discovered baseball cards in mint condition, old stamps by the sheets, also in mint condition, so many things of high value that you never knew what you were going to find. And then one day as I was cleaning out a back bedroom closet, I pulled out a box and as I started to go through it, I came across a large tin box. Wondering what could be in it, I opened it up. Immediately I screamed and ran out of the room to get Jack and Gayle.

"You both have to come, you are not going to believe what is in this box! Hurry, hurry! Jack, you open it up." He looked at me with an expression of wondering whether or not he should open it. Then he said, "Is something going to jump out at me? I don't trust you!" With a smile on my face, I told him, "No! You are not going to believe it!!"

I've always heard stories of people finding treasures in attics and such, but never really believed I would find one—but I had. Inside this box of money there was a note that said one word, "ENJOY" and it was signed, Jackie. There were $175,000 dollars in this tin box! We all started to laugh and cry at the same time. Amazing! What a silver lining that was for Jack.

We had some yard sales, donated a bunch of stuff to various charities, and hired a cleaning crew to come in and get the house ready to put on the market. Then we went back home and did the same thing with Jack and Gayle's home, the pottery shop, and our apartments.

On July 1st, everyone who was going to move with us to Copallis, Washington, packed their camping gear into the van and headed to the Coast so they could see with their own eyes what they were moving to.

There were Jack, Gayle, me, Steven, Roy, Tim, Georgie, and Thomas and maybe Chris. None of us were too keen on Thomas, but he had wheedled himself into Gayle's life. We could never understand what it was about this "conniving queen" that Gayle found so wonderful. But we went along with the flow, thinking we could just pretend he wasn't there. We all wanted a new adventure and a new beginning, and we could overlook some things. Or so we thought. Besides that, who were we to complain? Hadn't she took all of us under her wing, just as we were, with all our hang-ups and drama's?

We had a wonderful time and surprisingly everyone got along really well. Even the weather cooperated by being warm and sunny. Everyone was ready to commit to Jack and Gayle and the relocation of the pottery shop. But there was a bombshell waiting for me when I got home!

Chapter 29

"Mom, don't yell, but," . . . Words you never want to hear from your teenager. "I think I am pregnant."

"Oh Marie, why didn't you guys use protection?" I wanted to yell, but I didn't. I could see in her beautiful blue eyes that she was scared and just needed me to listen and most of all to hug her. I was too trusting and so caught up in my own life, that I was really not even paying attention to Marie and Bob. I felt pretty bad that because of my own selfish needs, I hadn't been there for the most important person in my life, my daughter.

"Marie, what do you want to do? You have options, but I don't want to be the one raising your child. I will help, but I am still going to move to the coast."

"Oh no, mom, we want to get married."

I looked at Bob and he said, "Susie, you know how much I love Marie. We do want to get married. My job is here, and my parents are here, so if we need help, they will be there for us." Oh gee, thanks a lot! I wanted to say that, but didn't.

Isn't it interesting that when you look back at key areas of your life, you see things so differently? I should have had a private talk with my daughter, to see where she really was with this. But I hadn't. So in a way I had forced her into a marriage that I wouldn't find out till much later, she didn't want to be in. Marie felt she had no other choice.

Geeze!!! When was this life going to not be about me, but put others first, instead of always being about me, me, me!

Everyone was moving to the coast the last week in August, and we all helped in loading the U-Hauls. My stuff was the last to pack up. And because I was in the middle of throwing a wedding together, I kept only the bare essentials. The day after the wedding in

September, my friend Sharon, packed up the rest of my stuff in her truck and towed my car which was also packed. We finally left Spokane, headed west, and I was ready to start my new life. Oh, what a beautiful future I had envisioned, all of us sharing our lives, working at the pottery shop, living at the ocean—wow! This was really going to be cool.

Here's where those "rose-colored glasses" come in. What was I thinking? Love, peace, tranquility? Not with an instigator in the mix, Thomas! The only one who liked him at all was Gayle, and they seemed to be stuck together like glue, and then there was Jack . . . I guess Jack was under the impression that he had all this "free help" and could put people on a schedule, and be in charge of telling these adults what to do and when, sort of like a foreman.

First of all, Jack had no tact, and because of this, there was no way anyone was going to take orders from Jack, and secondly, it seemed that Thomas was "excused" from doing any work of any kind, like doing dishes, dusting or even cleaning the bathtub after he had finished "his daily soakings."

Sharon and I hadn't even gotten into the school building when I was slammed with some very angry people! There is a saying in the gay community, "don't piss off a queen!" Well, I am here to tell you that is sooooo true! I finally said to them," Stop! You need to give me some time here, so let's call a meeting for the day after tomorrow, and we'll all sit down together and discuss our concerns, okay?" And then Tim said, "Okay, girlfriend, but just be warned, this is not going to be pretty!"

Oh boy, was he right. And why did they think I could figure this out? Why was I put into this mediator role?

You could cut the tension with a knife the minute the meeting was called. Every person there was very agitated except for Gayle and Thomas. Hmm . . . . what a mess this was. And the bulk of the problems were centered around being told what to do by Jack, and that not everyone was included. Thomas did not have to do any of the household task's, or work in the pottery shop. The fact that Gayle was totally wrapped up with this person, was causing very big problem, not with just all of us, but also with Jack.

By March of 1997, most of the people had left. Jack being what they call a brittle diabetic was not doing well, and I was off to Spokane for the birth of my grandbaby. While I was there I also met with my attorneys and learned that our case would be heard the second week of April. Finally!

While I was there, I stayed at my dad's place for a few days. He was not doing well at all. He had heart disease, was on medication, and still drinking.

"Dad, you have to stop this, you are going to kill yourself!" I would almost be yelling at this point. And I remember him saying, "Oh, honey, it's not that much, it's okay." AHHHHH, I truly wanted to pull my hair out. At least he was much more mellow in his old age of sixty-eight than when we were growing up with a violent and abusive alcoholic father.

I was staying with my dad and his second wife, Jackie, when the trial started and then I was able to see just how bad off he was. My sister, Julia, was going to be my 'caregiver'. For her this was basically making sure I would be getting back and forth from court safely and making sure I had a good lunch. I wasn't to know exactly how important this would become.

I'd also decided that I couldn't stay at the pottery shop any longer, and planned that when I made it back there, I would put everything in storage, and deal with it after the trial. I was not expecting to find everything in such disarray as it was. Steven and Roy were moving into Aberdeen, a town where our doctors were located, and wanted me to move there too. I thought that was a good idea.

The idea of this co-op of people working together for the shop, and our own piece of mind, just didn't turn out as we had expected, and I couldn't figure it out. There had to be more to it than Thomas. It was my very special friend, Steven, who finally took off my rose-colored glasses and said, "Suswah (my nickname), haven't you noticed Gayle's behavior? Haven't you noticed her relationship with Thomas? Haven't you noticed how she is treating Jack? Haven't you noticed . . . . ?" By the time Steven and Rob were finished telling me, I was crying. I had lost my best friend to cocaine, and she and Thomas had become drug-buddies. They had also gone through a lot of money in the process. It made a lot of sense once it was pointed out to me. I had never been around this drug so I had no reference to it.

"Is that why she has been losing all this weight?" Their answer was yes.

I told Jack and Gayle that when I got back from the trial I, too, would be moving into Aberdeen and that if Jack still wanted me to work in the shop, I would like that, too.

Jack responded, "I don't know how much pottery I'm going to be throwing, since I won't have anybody helping with the shows and stuff." He was looking right at Gayle when he said that, and she just got up and walked away. Jack was on the verge of tears, and I began to cry. Oh, how sad it was. Jack and I hugged each other. He was truly a broken man. That was the last time I ever saw him—this weird little man who could throw the most beautiful pottery I've ever seen!

Chapter 30

I was settled in at my dad's place. He looked so tired, more so even than the last time I was here and that was only ten days ago. Julia helped me pick out what outfit I would be wearing and checked to see that I had all my meds with me, and accompanied me to my last meeting with my attorneys before the trial on Monday. She also needed to know what would be going on in court so there would be no surprise reactions from her that the jury might read something into. We were set for trial April 10th 1997, at 9 AM in the Spokane County Court House.

"THE COURT MAY COME TO ORDER"

To say that I was a little nervous was an understatement! And after the opening statements were read, I was the first person called. I cried through most of my testimony, which I knew I would. I was really a bundle of nerves, and that's what the jury was seeing: A frightened woman with HIV, telling her story to the courts, and soon to be adding her voice to the millions around the world who have been screaming to be heard. We wanted our laws to protect us from "the infected" who knowingly infected us, and now could be held accountable for spreading a deadly and infectious disease.

Even though we were going "in the back door" to do this, also known as a civil case and not criminal, it would still set law, being that this is the Department of Corrections for Washington State, and a parole officer, David Bowman, held as liable, the definition of liable is the crux of this case: Liable implies a possibility or probability of incurring something because of position, nature, or a particular situation.

This would go back to Joe's DOC file being 'red flagged', when he was first paroled into the public when David Bowman first met me, and the manner in which I was introduced to him by Joe. It would include my complete file of medical records that Dr. Ruark had, to my current medical records from my current doctor, Dr. Susan Cophner, as well as my records from the CDC, which had gone through my file from Dr.Ruark with a fine-tooth comb.

This was very important for several reasons. One, they were able to determine exactly when I became infected. Two, they were able to cross-check the blood type of his disease to mine and to prove they were related, that is, our diseases had an origin, and mine was related to Joe's as its source. If others were found to be infected by Joe, their disease could be typed to see if it had an origin with Joe's. And the attorneys had spent a great deal of time and money in attempting to locate other women that were. We were able to find one, and were still looking for the girlfriend he was with before he went to prison. We knew who she was, Amber Stewart, and that she had moved from Spokane, and that was it. But Charlene Weaton did come forward.

This was the last place Charlene wanted to be and she had asked to be brought forward only as a last resort. No one in her life knew she had HIV, including family, job, and friends, and once she took the stand, it would become public knowledge. My heart really went out to Charlene, another victim at the hands of Joe, and I remember that the prosecuting attorney in my criminal case had called him a predator. How fitting that description was, I felt much better that he was in a place where he couldn't infect anyone anymore.

Then I was asked a question that really dumbfounded me.

"Ms. Wyatt, if there is a judgment of monies in this case, what will you do with it?"

Wow, I had really never even thought about it. I was so focused on the legal aspect, and I certainly wasn't putting myself through all this, for money!

"Considering the extent of my medical care, it's very expensive to keep me alive, and I am very thankful that my government thinks I am worth it. So I guess some of the money would take care of that.

Also I would give monies to the Spokane Aids Network which has been there for me from the first time I reached out for help."

I was the type of person who kept a pocket calendar, and in that calendar I wrote down all my appointments and remarks concerning them. It really was important because I had so many appointments for therapy for my back injury, for dates for lunch with friends, when I met Joe, my date with my son to go play darts, a variety of things. I always did this, and they were trying to enter it into evidence as proof of when I met Joe, and what transpired from that point on.

The State's Assistant Attorney General would be the DOC's attorney, and boy, oh boy, was he ever threatening. I was cross-examined by a man who had a very deep voice, used his hands to gesture as he talked, and seemed to be very angry with me. Everything about me was put through the wringer. Here is how some of his questioning went:

"So, Ms. Wyatt, you have had many sexual partners, is that correct? So, Ms. Wyatt, how many times did you and Joe have sex? How many times in a day, what kind of sex did you have? Any whips and chains? Any multiple partners?"

This was totally humiliating and unnecessary. They were doing whatever they could to discredit my reputation and character, and it finally ended with the judge making the Attorney General move on from this line of questioning.

By the time we broke for lunch, I could hardly eat anything that Julia had packed for us. Instead I spent most of the time quietly crying. I was so embarrassed by what had taken place I couldn't even look at myself in the mirror. Thank God for my sister. She was my rock. And she kept me on track as to why I was going through all of this—not only for myself, but for all the people who didn't have a voice. I just felt so embarrassed and humiliated! And now everyone had all my secrets of our sex life, including my sister.Soon it would be reported in the newspapers, and maybe even be on the nightly news on TV! OH MY GOD!

By the time court was over that first day, my testimony was over, and I was drained and sick to my stomach. Even though there was plenty of media present, I did no on-camera interviews while this case was being heard. The reporters could talk to the attorneys but not to me. But it didn't stop them from reporting on how I looked after being on the stand all day. And I looked awful, especially in their pictures. At least they never connected me to my son who had been found guilty of second-degree murder. That would have turned this case into a zoo, and I would have been judged on his merits, not mine.

I remember that when we showed up for court on day two there were about two dozen people out front of the court house with signs, and when they saw me, Julia, and my attorneys, a big cheer went up for us, with the media there taking pictures. Ah . . . . a group of supporters, wow! And then I saw the organizer of this group—my dear friend, Lynn. She waved and smiled and shouted at me, letting me know they were all there for me. "You go girl, for all of us!" Then Julia said in my ear, "See, I told you it was worth it!" Yeah, it was worth it.

My friend, Richard Lasater, was called to testify by the defense. It was brought out that when the DOC found out he was going to testify for me in court, they weren't too happy! And they couldn't shake him or threaten him from testifying. With Richard's testimony they lost their case.

On the fourth day of trial, Dr. Susan Cophner was called. She explained to the jury how this disease works in the body, and the damage it can do as well as all the different things we could be inflicted with. I listened to all of this and felt sicker and sicker as she went on to tell all the things I could potentially go through. But then she was asked a question that rocked my world, and the answer was even worse.

"Dr, Cophner," my attorney asked, "With your expertise in this field of HIV/AIDS, and treating many patients, do you have an educated opinion on what would Susan's life expectancy be?" My head raised, I turned around to make eye contact with Julia, feeling as though I were a deer caught in the headlights of a car, and waited for my doctor's response.

"Mr. Delmonico, to the very best of my knowledge and education, Susan will be very fortunate to see her fifith birthday." WWWHHHAAAT ! OH MY GOD! FIVE YEARS?

I WAS TOTALLY NOT READY FOR THAT! I turned white, and burst into a pool of tears, and felt all of what might be in my stomach coming up. I stood up and fled the courtroom to the nearest bathroom with my sister Julia in tow, and just barely made it to the nearest toilet, as everything in my being came up! And I was sobbing hysterically! The next thing I knew, I was lying on the tile floor and there was a sizeable crowd gathered around me in the bathroom! My sister, my doctor, my attorney and others I didn't know were there. I was in shock, and they were debating on whether or not I should go to the hospital. When I came to I was crying once again. It seems that I had been unconscious for several minutes, and I didn't want to go to the hospital, I just wanted to go home . . . . and that's exactly what I did, with instructions from my doctor to go straight to bed, and take the medication he handed me. Ah, come on, another pill? I chose some pot instead.

Friday was closing arguments, and I just sat there, very weak from the previous day, trying not to get too worked up. By afternoon the case was given to the jury, and we all went home. I would be notified when the jury had reached their verdict.

I was exhausted physically, mentally, and emotionally. I was so glad it was over. The trial had taken a lot out of me, and when my five-year life expectancy was factored in, I really wondered not only how long I was really going to live, but in what condition, and also where I was going to live. How could I change all of this? I don't want to die, I want to live! And I want to live a long life! I wanted to see my grandson grow up. I DON'T WANT TO DIE!!! Right then and there I decided that after this was truely all over with, I would go on a journey to find the answer. This would be something I not only physically needed to do but my soul needed to do it, too. We needed to do this together. Not only would there be a silver lining to all of this but there would be some jewels along the way, too. Some amazing full circles. But it was to take years.

"Has the jury reached a verdict?" The judge asked, his booming voice reverberating throughout the court room.

I was so ready for this to be over with! I just wanted to get on with my life, for however long I had, and I was damn sure going to do whatever I could to extend my life, and the quality of whatever that new life was going to be was a number one priority. That was what I was thinking about when the jury foreman stood and said in a soft but firm voice, "Yes, your honor we have."

I couldn't understand why my attorneys seemed saddened by the news. Didn't I hear that they found the State guilty? I had a smile on my face—what had I missed?

"Why are you angry, Jim? We won, didn't we?" I whisper.

"Susan, I am so sorry, but they didn't award any money."

"Yeah, but they were found guilty, right? They were found culpable, right?" I said in a small voice.

"Yes, they were, but they are saying that you should have protected yourself. That because you were sexually active you take the responsibility of protecting yourself, not the State." Jim said with sadness in his voice.

I frankly wasn't that concerned about the money. It was how the jury came to that conclusion. I became infected, according to the CDC, the latter part of August 1992. I had met David Bowman the first part of July 1992, and been introduced to him as Joe's girlfriend. That is when I should have been told the truth. Whether I stayed with Joe or chose to wear protection after that point would have been my responsibility. But at least I wouldn't have been infected. As they say, "You just never know what the jury will do ".

Either way, this case did set precedent. Laws were changed. And this case and the files from the criminal case could be used to further the cause which was, that if you know that you have a disease, and you do not relay this information to someone who could potentially contract the disease from you, you can be brought up on charges, and face a sentence of up to life in prison. Not a pretty picture. But now I could finally breathe. It was over and now I could get on with the rest of my life.

As we were coming out the courthouse doors, microphone's were pushed into my face. Questions were yelled at me. But what I heard was cheers in the back of this crowd of reporters. Ah, my supporters, and it put a smile on my face, and then I remembered what

I had just gone through. Julia was right, this was for all of us, those who wouldn't have a voice, I spoke for them. Those who couldn't go through this court zoo! So what if everyone now knew of Joe's and my sexual desires. I had the choice of what these reporters were going to focus on and it wasn't going to be sex! It was going to be about HIV! How it's spread. Who's at risk.(which is everyone) and that now, people who knownly spread this disease will be held liable in a court of law.

I will always live with the fact that I didn't think enough of myself to use protection. I didn't think that a woman, 40 years old who wasn't very sexually active, had to think of something like HIV/AIDS invading her life! Or of the damage and shame of having HIV, and the subsequent effects on my family. I will always be poor financially, but that is just a by-product. It's what I do with the rest of my life that will define me and continues to do so to this day. But I chose a hard path, and for a long time I didn't have very good light to see my way on this path.

Chapter 31

By the time I arrived at my dad's place, the news was on and this case was a featured story. They were watching my interview and also my attorney's, and of course, the reporters' commentary. My dad was not happy that they didn't award any money.

"But dad, we set law with this case! I said "Don't you know how important that was? It's the whole case!"

Well, you can't live on that, Susan! And you sure as hell can't eat it! What are you going to live on, welfare?"

It was at this point that I realized my dad had had more than his usual "one drink." And if I have learned anything from my childhood, it was to never argue with a drunk!

"We'll talk tomorrow, Dad. Right now I am very tired." So I just kissed him on the cheek, and went to bed.

The next morning as I was packing to leave Joan, Dad's wife, asked me if I could come back over in a couple of weeks. She was a bartender, and was going to be closing up the bar for a few weeks and wanted to know if I could keep an eye on dad. I never thought I would be asked to babysit my dad, but I could tell he wasn't doing very well at all in addition to his drinking.

"Yes, I can do that. I have to go put my stuff in storage, and then I'll be back. But I need to know how bad Dad really is. I think both of you have been sugar-coating his health." I said this with worry and a bit of anger too.

"Well," Joan said, "The doctors have said that his congestive heart disease is worse and he has confusion sometimes. Oh, and sometimes he is a bit dizzy. Oh, and sometimes he is short of breath."

I guess I let out some of the anger I had been holding in. "And he is still drinking?" I yelled. I was totally pissed off!

"Oh, honey, it's not that much." That, coming from a bartender and a drinker herself!

Yeah, right. I took a deep breath and said with as much control as I could muster, "Joan, he shouldn't be drinking at all, he has to stop."

"Oh, I couldn't do that. We always have a cocktail or two at night. I can't take that away from him."

AHHHH! I just wanted to scream! I realized at that point that taking Dad's booze away really wasn't going to help. The damage was probably already done. So I contacted his primary doctor, Dr. Ruark, who had been my doctor, too, and let him know how much Dad was really drinking. He said he suspected as much and that no, there was really nothing I could do about it. He also let me know that my dad's health was not good, and that he should be watched as much as possible. As Julia was taking me to the bus station, I let her know about dad, and she said she would be checking in on him, too.

I settled back in my bus seat, and was really glad that the bus was only about half full. That way I would have the seat next to me empty, maybe all the way to Olympia. Ah, that would be great! From there I would get on another bus to Aberdeen, then another one to Copallis Beach, and then home. Even if I was going back to pack up my belongings and put them in storage, I could figure out later exactly where I was going to move. I really didn't want to move back to Spokane, and I really liked going down to the ocean whenever I wanted, so I was pretty much settling on Aberdeen.

I was going to miss the pottery shop, and my old friend Gayle (Millie). Maybe, I thought, she had stopped using the drugs and everything would be how it was supposed to be. Maybe when I got there everything would be okay. And then I heard a still, quiet little voice in my head, "Yoo-hoo, Miss Rose-Colored Glasses, not going to happen, so think about something you can do—a little reality here, please!" My trip home on the bus was perfect! And quiet, yeah, no crying kiddies, and no loud talkers, only music, perfect. Then KABOOM!

Chapter 32

It was dark by the time I got home, and I went straight to my apartment, took a shower and then went to bed. When I got up in the morning, I could see that someone had been in my apartment and some of my things taken. All the fish in the 50-gallon tank were dead, and the pump was gone. What was going on?

I found Jack in the shop and stopped dead in my tracks. He looked awful!

"Jack, what's going on? You look terrible!"

"Ah, it's nothing; they just changed my diabetes medications, he said with a little laugh. "It will work out soon. I heard you get in last night. Sorry about your car, Susie."

"What! What do you mean, my car?"

I ran out of the pottery shop and down the hall, and burst through the doors to the parking lot. I started screaming, as I saw my little red car, completely smashed! Totaled! OH MY GOD! What happened? Who did this? And then I started crying. What am I going to do without a car? I crumpled to the ground and just started sobbing. It was sort of like the straw that broke the camel's back. Jack was the only one here with me, and he didn't know what to do. After about five minutes we went back to my apartment.

Jack handed me a pot pipe and I quickly calmed down and stopped crying

"Jack, what happened to my stuff here? And where is Gayle?"

"It's a good thing you are stoned, Susie, because things have changed around here, and I don't know what I am going to do." Jack began to cry, something I never thought I would see. He had lost his wife to Thomas and cocaine, and I had lost my very best friend.

Packing up my stuff was not a fun event. I cried throughout. With help from my case manager, Andy, I was able to find a storage unit and all my possessions went into it. When I come back in a couple of weeks, I was to contact Andy and at that time he would help me find a place to live. This wasn't in his job description, but he was that kind of person.

I stayed with Steven and Roy that night and we sat around and talked about a dream gone wrong. The next morning they took me to Olympia, on my way to Spokane, to keep an eye on my dad. And I was looking forward to spending time with him. I hoped he was doing better than the last time I'd seen him, about ten days ago.

Chapter 33

"Wow, dad, you look pretty good!" I said with a smile, even though he didn't look so great. It wasn't any one thing you could pinpoint. But he looked tired, and was slow in movement. It was even hard for him to get out of his chair.

"Ah, honey, I'm not doing so well, but I think it's the new medicine the doc has me on."

I went and checked over his medications, and the first thing I noticed was that almost all of them had a warning of NO ALCOHOL.

"Hey, dad, did you know that most of these medications say not to drink alcohol? Did you know that? Are you still drinking?" I said with my voice filled with trepidation because I knew what he was going to say

"Well, Susie, I have cut way back."

Sometimes you just have to shake your head and let it go. Dad and I did spend some quality time together, for which I was very thankful. Actually, it was the first time I can remember that we ever had.

About a week later, around two AM, I woke up to a voice screaming my name and I went barreling out of bed into the hallway. There lying on the floor was my dad. I screamed at Joan to call 911. Dad had had a massive heart attack, and no amount of CPR was going to help. He was gone, and Joan stayed drunk as a skunk for the next several days.

I Left the day after the funeral. I needed to get back to my life and to find a place to live. Funny thing, it finally hit me that for the first time in my life, I was homeless and carless. Man, was this spiral downward in my life going to hit bottom anytime soon? I really didn't think I could take very much more. You know the saying,

"God doesn't give us more than we can handle?" HELLO, GOD, ARE YOU THERE? NO MORE! I HAVE HAD IT! OKAY?

As I was traveling back to Olympia, this time on the train, I made up my mind that I was going to find a way to locate that "silver lining." Now that both of my parents were gone, I had no one to help me and for the very first time, I really felt alone. So I proceeded to have a conversation with myself, and my journey to find my spiritual path of enlightment, and self-healing was born.

However, I was not finished with the bombshells in my life, and by the time 1998 rolled around, my best friend, Steven, had moved back to Spokane, and I was beginning to have very serious health problems.

Chapter 34

In 1999, I had carved out a quiet life for myself in Aberdeen Washington. I was still having a lot pain from these boils. I spent a lot of time getting books from the library, watching Oprah, and riding the bus out to many different spots along the beach. I can honestly say that Aberdeen, Washington, had the best public transit system of any place I have been.

I also had an attorney who was trying to get me on permanent disability status. I thought it was for my back injury, but he was going for my status of HIV.

The one bright spot in all of this was the day in March when I answered my door, and it was Steven. Steven! I yelled and hugged him at the same time. This was amazing and we talked and talked. I was so glad he had left Roy. He stayed with me for several days. I told him of the awful pain I was having and what I had been doing. Shortly afterward, Steven left to go see his friends who lived in and ran a spiritual retreat. He came back several days later, and he looked as though he was glowing, really.

"Wow, Steven, you look great! What's going on?"

"Suswah (the nickname he had given me), I have fallen in love! But I knew it before I went out there. I went out there to see Les; I was led to find him!" And Steven started to cry! Yes! Happy tears! FINALLY!

Around June of 1999, I was in serious pain from all the boils that were breaking out all over my body, in my armpits, and on my breasts. They were huge, oozing, smelled horrible, and no amount of anti-biotics were helping.

I was to the point that I didn't really care if I died. I didn't really tell my family the extent of my pain. Why would I? They couldn't help me, even all the doctors didn't know what to do except just give me more pills. I was sure that this one last doctor would know what the infection was and make it go away, because I really couldn't take any more.

So I got ready to see yet another doctor, and was in a very fragile state. It took a lot of time to even put a bra on, pack it with lots of gauze pads or even menstrual pads to soak up the infection, and the smell was sickening. I was a mess!!! And this infection, whatever it was, was killing me. All they would tell me was, "it must be an AIDS-defining infection!"

I have found that if the experts didn't know what something was, and they knew you had HIV/AIDS, well, that had to be it. So anything unknown automatically went into the category of an AIDS-defining illness. My lab work at the time showed that my T-cells were falling dramatically, which told the doctors that whatever this infection was, it was not good.

"Well, Ms. Wyatt, I would like you to take this antibiotic, and come back in two weeks," the doctor said.

Sorry to say, I totally lost it. I began to cry, and said in a rather loud voice, "If this infection was in your balls, you would be doing more than taking an antibiotic, sir!

This will be my eighth time, taking another antibiotic, as you well know because it's in my file, of taking pills that aren't working!!!!"

I ran out of his office crying, and walked home. I was in a really bad state. By the time I got home, I was drained. All I wanted to do was take my pain pills, take a bath, and go to bed.

The phone was ringing as I was came through the door, and as I answered it, I had no idea this phone call was to change my life.

Chapter 35

I really wasn't going to answer the phone. I didn't want to put on a "happy voice" in case it was my daughter, or other family and friends.

"Oh, everything is great, doing good, tell me how's everything with you?" Something like that. I was really tired of living the "poor little Susie" syndrome. Even though I really had a serious and painful health problem, I was just tired of there always being this carousel ride of drama that I just couldn't get off. There was always something that would focus on me. Yea, 'poor little Susie': "You believe what has happened to her again!" Or, "What's going to happen to her next, poor thing." Or," I don't know how much more she can take." So I tried lately to be upbeat when family called. I was tired of all the attention and I didn't want to burden my family. But for some unknown reason, I answered the phone.

"Hi Andy, (my client advocate here in Aberdeen) no, I just got home . . . . Just wanted me to take another antibiotic and return in two weeks . . . . Didn't know what it is. Yeah, I'm home for the day. Going to take some pain medication, have some tea. Why? Well, I could really use some good news. Yeah, come on over. Okay, see you in a bit."

When Andy came in he gave me a great big hug, but not too tight. He had a huge smile on his face and just glowed! I wondered if there would come a time in my pathetic (woops, pity-party thought!) life when I would glow like that.

"Susie, there is a hospital up in the Seattle area called Virginia Mason Hospital, and they have a whole wing of the hospital dedicated to HIV/AIDS research and treatment. I talked to the medical administrator about your infection. And they want to see you tomorrow. I can take you up there. So what do you say, yes?"

YES YES YES! Oh God, please, let there be some answers! Maybe, just maybe the answers will be there, and maybe I will finally be pain free! Please!

I called Steven and told him the news and he and Les came over with a pizza and we talked. They told me there was going to be a Reiki group meeting in a couple of days and that I should come and get worked on.

"What the heck is Reiki? And what do you mean, worked on?"

They both laughed and told me that many people are involved in this form of healing others of many different things, by using their own energy and power to find the dis-ease-ment in someone and be able to pull that negativity out of them and sweep it away. It helps if you yourself believe yourself that this can be done. But the person performing Reiki always has to have the permission of the "patient." Okay, I thought, I'm game. I have nothing to lose except this ugly, smelly, painful infection, yeah, and I was open to this.

And getting worked on means you lay on a table as if you were getting a massage. Then a licensed Reiki

Master will go into a meditation and guide his hands slightly above your body without really touching you and focus in on any medical issues you may have. Some Reiki Masters can even remove blockages of pain which dwell in the recesses of the mind.

Jesus had said that we all are physicians and have the ability to heal ourselves, if we just believed. Wow! Could this really be true? This would become not only a silver lining in my life, but the beginning of my spiritual path to find wholeness and joy, and to live with a forgiving heart, for myself and for others.

It was a two-hour drive up to Seattle on a good day. We had to be there by 9 AM so I was up at 6 getting ready—very early for me. And I was having a bad day as it was. I had thrown up my meds and what little else was in my stomach. So I munched on crackers in the car.

I had never been in a hospital this big. No wonder they give you a map when you check in at the front desk. It was a good thing that Andy knew where we were going, because I was pretty foggy upstairs. I didn't know if it was the pain medicine or the infection.

I was beginning to have trouble focusing on things and forgetting a lot. I just chalked it up to the meds I was on, because, what if I had what Joe had? No way, don't go there Susie! Don't think like that! Shhhh, I was almost 50.

I was finally seated in a beautiful waiting room. We were nine stories high and there was a breathtaking view of Seattle and the pier. Surprisingly it was a sunny, blue-sky day, and that was a real bonus. I wish I could have eaten some of the food that was laid out in a buffet arrangement on a side table. The fruit looked very inviting as well as all the different kinds of pastries. But I knew that it would just come back up. Maybe later.

Chapter 36

"Hi Susan, I'm Dr.Abuloffeia. Do you have another name you would like me to use?" Wow, now that was a change. Very good bed side manner.

"Yes, you can call me Susie. It sounds a little happy, and I hope you can make me feel that way again. I'm so tired. Please make me well." And I started to cry. Just to be able to release all this built-up sadness and pain was really overwhelming for me.

The doctor just sat quietly with me until I stopped crying, about ten minutes later. Now what doctor has the time or empathy to do that? Yeah! I was in a good place.

"Now, let's see what we are dealing with." After my examination, Dr. A (it was easier to say, so that was his name I gave him) left the room and told the nurse to take me to the lounge, also known as the waiting room, He also had given me an injection that would allow me to eat something and keep it down.

"I am going to run some tests on this infection, and as soon as you have eaten some food and it stays down, you will be going to get a CAT scan and an ultra-sound, okay? The good news is, I think I know what this is, but I have never seen it this bad. We will talk in about ninety minutes. Don't worry, Susie, we will take care of this infection, once and for all! Okay."

Okay? Oh yeah! Finally! And don't you know, I went straight for the pastries, and they stayed down! Ah, that felt good. I want to get some of that stomach medicine. It also made me feel a little high and my pain was almost all gone. Wow, what else had he given me? I was definitely going to find out, that is, if I was able to remember.

A couple of hours later, I was in Dr. A's office with Andy. He was to take notes for me because I was afraid I would forget something important, a situation that was happening more and more frequently.

"Susie, what you have is a MRSA-type infection. It has not only caused mastitis in both breasts, but it has started to spread to the brain. That is why you have started to forget things and are having problems recalling. It's not dementia, and I believe we can reverse the damage because it is fairly new up there in the brain and hasn't really taken hold. But given another month, we would be looking at a very serious situation. But it has caused very severe damage, and the only way we can get rid of this infection is to remove it surgically. That's the good news. The bad news is . . . .

I am very sorry, Susie, But to insure that we get all of the infection, we will need to remove your breasts, and possibly some lymph nodes," Dr. A said with great sadness in his voice and on his face, and all I could do was smile.

"You mean, I can once and for all be rid of this pain? By taking off my breasts? Is that what you are telling me?" I was almost giddy. Dr. A was very baffled by my reaction as he said yes.

Cool! "How soon?" I remember asking him. I thought it was time to tell this beautiful and caring man in front of me that I had been lugging these 42 double-D's around most of my life, and if it meant getting rid of them in order to be painfree . . . . Oh Yeah! I can do that. NO problem. No, I don't want reconstruction, either. I was afraid that it might come back. Even though they said it was quite unlikely, I wasn't going to take any chances. And to this day I have never, never, regretted that decision.

It took several months before the CAT scan came back clear of infection. Boy oh boy, as they say, I dodged the bullet on that one. Or was it the Reiki? And a bit of strangeness in this was that I was scheduled to stay in the hospital for ten days. I was released in thirty-six hours! There was NO infection in my body and this totally shocked the doctors! I had told Dr. A that I had a Reiki treatment before I came up for surgery, and the funny thing was, he knew exactly what that was!

Dr. A also told me that this was indeed an AIDS-defining infection, and because my T-cells were below 100—a healthy person's count is around 1200—I was now classified with AIDS. The thing that was floating around my brain was that if Reiki could work on this infection and the doctor's skill had removed the damaged tissue, well maybe, just maybe, I could finally heal some really ugly scars in my life. Ah! Could I finally be on the right track? Could things finally be turning around in my life? Let's see, from 1992 till the end of June, 1999 . . . . Well, if this could really be happening, it's about damn time. Talk about a slow learner! I was now forty-nine years old, and I was committed to proving Dr. Cophner's estimate of my life expectancy wrong! I was going to live well past fifty!

So with Home Health Care and a nurse to check on me every day, and help at home, they let me go home. And for the first time, in a long, long time, I was pain-free!!!!! And it felt soooo good!

Chapter 37

Steven or Les, or both of them, would come over to see me every day, and we would talk about our lives, where we wanted to be and how to achieve a life of spiritual joy and peace in our lives and in our surroundings. And how living in a specific area can help or hinder that journey. But most of all, how to get rid of the "old programming" in our brains and hearts. I wanted to walk my truth. I wanted to live my truth. I wanted to be able to look back on my life and see change! I wanted to be able to speak from wisdom! I wanted to be an authentic person! It seemed I was ready to make some dramatic changes in my life. Some would say they were quite overdue!

Les and Steve brought over plenty of books and videos to occupy my time. Wow! I had never read books like these. Not only were they books on how to change my life but on how to meditate, how to heal, how to remove old teachings—also known as brainwashings—and replacing them with self-love, self-forgiving, and my soul's journey here on this earth, and what I was here to learn. HEY! Were these silver linings or were they jewels that I was about to acquire for my crown? Ha, time would tell.

Then one day the attorney who was handling my disability claim called and said that we had a hearing in front of the judges to see if I qualified for a permanent disability. I was ready for that, and thinking I was going to be awarded benefits on my back injury, I was very surprised that I received my disability on my AIDS-DEFINING INFECTION which had caused me to have my breasts removed. This was a real gift, because now I would never have to worry about my medical situation, and I received a larger amount of money than what I was getting on welfare. Getting by would always be a struggle but now, ah, not as much. Yeah, I had some breathing room. I could now save some monies for my trips on the train or bus to visit Marie and my grandbaby, or my friends and other family.

I went out to the Wynoche River which was about fifteen miles where I lived, to visit Les and Steven. I planned to spend several days there. It was just beautiful, everything you could picture living next to a river. Les had just bought a 36-foot motor home that they were living in. He also had a 24-foot teepee that was fully finished inside. There was a one-room living area with a bed, a wood stove in the middle, a small kitchen complete with table and chairs, and over in another area were some rocking chairs and a table with a lamp. I saw a stereo in one area with new-age type music and Native American music. This was really cool and I definitely didn't want to leave.

One day while we were taking a hike up the river, Les and Steven informed me that they were going to be leaving soon. They were going to head south and find a permanent place to live. I took in a deep breath of shock. Oh no! Please don't leave, I said to myself, thinking only of myself. I didn't want my "brothers" to leave. They were all I had here!

Then Les asked, "Susie, would you consider moving with us?"

Would I? "Oh hell, yeah! Are you sure? Do you mean it?" I screamed as I hugged them and danced around them. This was just amazing. That night at dinner they laid down their travel plans. When they found a place, they would call me and let me make arrangements to come and check it out for myself, and see if I wanted to live where they landed.

Steven and I had talked about the pitfalls when all of us moved with Jack and Gayle to Copallis Beach, and we didn't want to make the same mistakes. Or were they mistakes? We didn't want to be locked into others' expectations and we needed to be free to be ourselves. We were all on a journey of finding our own spirituality and a path of peace, and also to put all we had learned, easy or hard, short path or a lifelong road, into practice. The boys would be on the road in a few days, and I would be in Aberdeen, working on my life, and waiting for their call. I knew it could be a long time before I would be packing up my stuff and moving somewhere, but not knowing where or when didn't bother me at all because I knew at least I would be in a place I needed to be.

I cleaned out every nook and cranny, packed all I could live without for a while, and got rid of a lot of stuff. It kept me busy and gave me something to do. Then one day I came home from dropping off some items at a thrift store and saw a strange car in my drive way, and people in my house! What was this all about? My front door opened and here came my friend Lynn, from Spokane. "Oh My God, Linnie," I screamed as we fell into each other's arms.

"The door was unlocked and I knew you wouldn't mind if we made ourselves at home," she said with a laugh."

"No, I don't mind at all! Why didn't you call" What are you doing here?" I said with a lot of concern in my voice, because my friend did not look good at all. She had lost weight, her hair was falling out, and she had just gotten over PCP (pneumocystis carinii pneumonia) which is a microorganism that attacks the interstitial tissue of the lungs, and is not only an AIDS-defining illness, but one that marks your time left on this earth.

"Susie, I don't have much time left, so I talked my caregiver, Vickie here, into driving over here and surprising you, and I want to see the ocean, Susie. I have never seen it. I want you and me to go to your favorite place, you know, the one you sent me pictures of. I want to spend the whole time with you. I also want to tell you how you changed my life!" She said all this with tears in her eyes and in her voice.

"Oh, Lynn, you're the one who gave me the strength to stand up and fight! You are the one who was out there in your wheelchair, in front of the courthouse with signs; you are the one who organized everyone to give my cases a platform and media exposure. You, my friend, are the one that gave me the badge of a survivor and not a victim. Oh Linnie, I love you, girl!"

You just never know when these jewels will show up in your life, but I had just completed a full circle in my life. This was one that I could see, and I cried like a baby when my friend left a few days later, for I knew I would never see her again, that is, in this lifetime. It seems we had meant a lot to each other. It's what they call soul-connected. She was meant to be in my life, even though it was for a very short eight years. My friend died two weeks later at home, with her family, while she was asleep, and painfree. Now that's the way to go, Lynn. Thank you for sharing your life with me. You, my friend, are my hero . . . .

Chapter 38

In June of 2000, the call came. "Hey, Susie, get your stuff packed, we found it! Do you want to come down and see it, or do you want us to just come up and get you?" The guys said it together and were laughing."

"Well, tell me about it at least!" By the time they were finished, well, it was time to come and get me.

"So how fast can you pack?" Les asked, and I started laughing because I was pretty much packed.

"How about tomorrow! I'm already packed!" And we all laughed.

By the end of June, I was all moved into our beautiful home in Klamath Falls, Oregon. This was a move that was going to impact all of us, and change our lives forever!

Wow! I was living in Oregon! The house was beautiful and had plenty of room for all of us, and we weren't in each other's way. I was learning to compromise. I didn't want a false illusion of us living together. In other words, I wanted all of us to be able to live together, and not fall apart like what happened in Copallis Beach.

We were only a few blocks from the downtown. We had never lived this close in a town, and it was kind of cool. I was within walking distance of the library, grocery store, farmers' market, and all the shops. Sometimes I would ride my bike and sometimes I would take the bus.

I could drive if I wanted to. I also discovered that an Amtrak train ran through town so I even had a way to go up north to see my family and friends. I loved traveling on the train and if you have the time, I would recommend it.

We also found a church that we were going to try out. All of us were done with man-made religion, and we were seeking something more on the spiritual path. After about three months we went to a meeting conducted by someone called Swami Ty. We wanted to see what he was all about.

It is really hard to put a definition on Swami. I asked him one time, early in our visits, "Swami, how would you describe yourself and your training in being a Swami?"

The first thing I learned was that Swami was a title as a teacher in the Hindu religious order where he had spent considerable time. Swami Ty began to describe himself.

"Well, let's see. I was born in the Native American culture of Shaman on my father's side, and Catholic on my mother's side. I traveled the world, learned many different religions, and settled on becoming a Swami because I liked the dress."

Ha, Ha, Ha! Yes, that was Swami.

"I have been everything and I have been nothing, just like you. You, Susie, have work to do, and by the way, your journey has been and will be a long one."

What? How did he do that? How did he know that? Well, I was hooked! And so were Steven and Les. This amazing man helped to mold me into the person I am today. But he was right; this was going to be an amazing journey and one that would last all of this lifetime here on earth.

The group that met with Swami twice a month was from all kinds of backgrounds, all ages, men and women. No subject was off limits. We talked about Atlantis to Lemuria, abductions to aliens, and Hopi prophecies to the Bible, meditation or prayer, UFOs to remote viewing. Like I said, everything. Many things I had never heard before, and he mentioned books, books, books. I would also tune into a talk-show radio station that was on from 10 PM to 2 AM at night, Coast to Coast AM with Art Bell, which later changed to Coast to Coast with George Nourey. Swami Ty also had a very unique way of teaching, because no matter how many questions you asked, he would respond with questions for you to find the answers to.

I was having a problem with this meditation or prayer thing, so one day I asked Swami what was the difference.

"Prayer is taking to God; meditation is listening to God, or that small, soft voice within you."

Oh, that made sense to me. So, I wondered, how do I meditate? And towards the end of our meeting he would lead all of us in meditation.

Another time I asked Swami, "I feel lost, Swami, when we are in meditation, and sending peace and love and light and protection to people in war-torn areas, like the Middle East or Africa or anywhere out there. I'm not getting it. I feel sad, but I don't see it. What am I missing?" And his answer to me will, I hope, show you how special this man had become in my life.

"When you meditate for others or for a situation that is affecting you, see it or them as if it is already accomplished. Example: you are sending safety or peace to the children in Mexico, living on the streets and eating out of dumps; picture them in the opposite, that they are safe, clean, and with healthy food to eat. See it already done. Same with governments, countries, even us! When we concentrate on a healing on ourselves we picture it already done, what it will look like healed, and how you would feel."

Well, that hit me like a ton of bricks!

"You mean, I can heal myself?"

And all he said was, "Yes, you can and here are some books for you to read." One of these books was Uri Geller's book called *Mind Medicine*, and another book was by Louise Hays, *Heal Your* Body.

We talked a lot about Reiki, chakras, body energy, healing crystals, breathing correctly and clearing blockages within our own energy flow. I was really absorbing all this new information. I realized that I was feeling better, life was good. I was finally growing.

Could this mean that I was finished with all the bombshells and kabooms, and I was finally making decisions that were good and healthy for me? Have I finally "seen the light"? Well, that depends, because I have come full circle in one sense, and was on to a new one. And all of this I have come to learn is for my soul's journey and what we need to learn, what I had to go through in my life to reach this stage in my life. Couldn't I have picked an easier way to get here? I guess not. I guess I needed to go through all this muck to make it to a path that had some light on it, and to share with others my life so maybe they won't have to make it so hard on themselves, or to let others know that there is help out here, and you don't have to be alone. To encourage you to go on. Look for that silver lining. Find a purpose and reason because it will be there. I hope that it won't take as long for you as it did for me, and that it won't be as painful. But please know this, that when you look back on your life, to look for hope and understanding and acceptance for what was, for that is where you will find the silver linings; that was where mine were.

Chapter 39

Les and I had decided that our front yard needed some tender loving, care. It needed a yard. It was pretty much a blank slate. We cleaned it up, planted grass and hollyhocks up by the house. Around the side of the house I was going to plant herbs. We had pigeons that roosted up on our roof and their poo piled up where I was going to plant. I thought that would be really good for my herbs so I got it all cleaned out and the space planted.

A couple days later I started not feeling very good, like I was coming down with the flu. Then the next day I wake up with headache, which was very unusual for me. As the day progressed, my neck started to get stiff and was a bit painful to turn to my left. A thought came into my head that I needed to get my medical book out and look up "meningitis". But I just shrugged it off like where did that thought come from. I told Steven and Les that if I didn't feel better in the morning I would call the doctor.

In the middle of the night I awoke from a sound sleep, and told to look up the word meningitis. I said to myself, okay, okay, knowing that I wasn't going to get any sleep until I did. I was so shocked! I had the same symptoms as those listed in my book. Wow!

I think that was the first time in my life that I listened to that small, soft voice within me, even though it woke me up in the middle of the night. In the morning I called my doctor. After giving her my symptoms and telling her what I suspected and about the pigeons, she told me to go to the hospital as soon as possible and she would meet me there.

Sure enough, I had contracted cryptococcosis meningitis. During this, my second hospital stay, I was treated pretty well even though they had not had too many HIV/AIDS patients come through. Klamath Falls was not a very big town. After several days I was able to go home. This could have been very serious, but because it was caught early, I dodged what could have been a bad and prolonged illness! Thanks to that small voice within me and acting on it, I was spared to go on with life.

The next morning, I came from the kitchen with my coffee, headed out to our front porch. I looked through the dining room windows and saw my adopted brother Les, in the front yard with a paint ball gun, which looks like a real gun, going around the house trying to scare the pigeons away. I started to laugh, went outside, and said, "Les, what the heck are you doing? You look like a madman out here with a gun! Someone is going to call the cops!!!!" Well, no sooner did I say that than a police car pulled up. I started to laugh hysterically, and the cop was telling Les to, "Sir, put the gun down!"

Well, then Les began to laugh, and the officer was not seeing any humor in this at all, and wasn't too happy with either one of us. I then explained that I just got home from the hospital and the pigeons were responsible for my stay, and that the gun was a paint gun, and that Les was just trying to make the pigeons go away. Now the more I was trying to tell this policeman what was going on, the harder Les and I were laughing. And then Steven came out of the house and said, "So, what's going on?" We were laughing so hard that tears were running down our faces. I think it was the first time I realized that "happy tears" don't hurt your eyes.

We could only imagine what kind of a story the cop would tell when he had to write up his report. I always wondered if he ever saw the humor in it. It still brings laughter to our story.

In October of 2001, my friend, Les' partner, and Pat's son, Steven died. He died of complications due to his hepatitis C condition. Steven died at home, surrounded by the three people who loved him the most. He also died pain-free, something that I promised him, for that was his biggest fear. My friend died a "good death", that is, he died in his sleep.

Steven always had a problem with getting ice out of the door of our refrigerator. There was always at least one ice cube that would spit out onto the floor that he would have to pick up. I never had that problem. Les never had that problem. But Steven did, almost every time he used it. It really became one of those things that you just had to laugh about.

It was a couple of months after Steven's death, Les was at work, I was downstairs watching TV. All of a sudden I heard ice falling to the floor in the kitchen. Not thinking, I screamed STEVEN! And went running up the stairs. As I rounded the corner to the kitchen, I realized what I was doing, and remembered that Steven was dead. I came into the kitchen and there were all of these ice cubes all over the floor. I fell to the floor and started laughing and said, "So you made it! It's about time you let us know." And then I started crying,

I remembered a time, eight years earlier, when my mom had given me a sign, a beautiful wild yellow rose bush, in the back yard of a cute little house I was about to rent. I thought to myself, you sure have come a long way, baby. Hmm, could this be another full circle in my life?

Chapter 40

Steven's death had been very fast, only 25 days, and sudden. Les and I settled down into a comfortable relationship of brother and sister, but here we had a six-bedroom house and there were just the two of us. Les had invited some friends of his down for a visit, Leela and Marge.

Les had also bought some property out of town, in the Bly Mountain area about thirty miles northeast of town. We named this place Spirit Meadow, put a little travel trailer out there, and spent lots of time on the property.

For us, Spirit Meadow was a magical place as well as beautiful. We had several trees that were over four feet across, like gentle giants. A seasonal creek ran through the meadow and the most beautiful wild flowers covering the meadow. There was this large but dead tree by our trailer that was the perfect 'trinket tree.' We started to decorate it with prayer bundles, hanging crystals and whatever we wanted to place in the arms of this magical tree. We also harvested some of the most wonderful wild sage and made smugging sticks.

It came about that Les had invited either one or both of the women to move in with us, to give them a new beginning, and in about two months Leela was all moved in. I really learned to compromise with her, and because of her, I later learned to set boundaries for myself. She was not an easy person to live with and I was really not liking this. Les was at work most of the time so he had very little contact with her.

Leela was a student of Ramtha and the School of Enlightment, up in Yelm, Washington, where she was from. She had spent lots of money on this and believed she was on a higher spiritual path than me. She also did not like Swami, and found ways to disregard things he would say.

One day we were all driving around outside of town. Les was looking for a house and property out in the rural area of Klamath Falls. Some people at the casino where he worked had told him to check out the location. As soon as we saw it, we knew we were going to move from the house in town and buy this home.

I had never lived out in the country and thought it would be cool. I could even raise chickens! But this place only had two bedrooms, and the situation with Leela were coming to a head. Les thought he could convert the attached garage into a bedroom, that is until Leela informed him that she wanted this, and this, and this, and her own bathroom—sort of like her own suite.

We bought the property out at Sprague River, and put the house in Klamath Falls on the market. We had made a lot of improvements to it and it sold in thirty days. There was going to be a lot of work to do at our new house before we moved in. We sanded down the wood floors and painted the whole house inside.

One day while Leela and I were painting, the straw that broke the camel's back occurred. I had had enough. She was saying some very negative things about Les and that maybe we should find our own place up in Yelm and move, and I could go to the School of Enlightenment, and be like her. I had totally lost it.

"What the hell are you talking about? I'm not going to move anywhere with you, I am even having problems living with you. You always find faults in me and feel you need to point them out . . . . all the time! I can't be around you anymore!" And I left and went in to our home in Klamath Falls. I was out on the back deck having tea when Les came home from work.

"What are you doing here, I thought you were out at Sprague River?" He said with a smile, and I broke down in tears.

"Bro, I think I am going to have to find a new place to live, I can't live with that woman!" I was sobbing. My dream, my life was blowing up in my face. How much more could I take? Just when I was getting my life on track and then, KABOOM!

"Susie, you need to calm down and tell me what happened. I don't want you to leave. What did Leela do?"

When I had told him all of it, and her motive to split us up and turn me into her "puppet", he started to laugh. "What are you laughing about, this is not funny!" I was a little pissed.

"Don't you realize, Susie, this is a real growing area for you. You stood up for yourself. You didn't let her badger you into a poor decision. I'm frankly very proud of you, and no, you are not leaving. I've known what Leela has been up to. Demanding this and that. Susie, I know she will be the one to leave."

Les and Swami had taught me about "desire, belief, and intent," and the power behind this. I really hadn't put it to the test until now. You state your desire, believe that it will happen and intend, see it 100% materialize, or done, so be it! This was like the book, The Secret, by Rhonda Byrne, which I would read years later. He talks about being the Master of your own life, and live a life of Joy and Bliss . . . . Ah yes, this can really happen.

So that is what Les and I did. Leela was leaving for Texas in a few days for her grandson's wedding and while she was gone we were going to be moving our stuff into our new house. We would intend that she would not be moving with us, and when she returned she would let us know.

I was so shocked because that is exactly what happened. When she returned from Texas she drove out to our new house where we were still moving in, and started crying the minute she got out of the car.

She told us, "I'm so sorry but I can't move out here. I need to go back to Yelm and be closer to my school."

It seems she had made arrangements to do just that while in Texas, and she was gone in a week. From that time on I am a total believer in the power of thought—consciousness and energy creating reality. You might remember the old saying, be careful what you wish for?

Chapter 41

Les had bought some "affirmation cards" and they really helped me to believe in myself, that I was important and I was valued. One of these cards, for an example, is: I let go of the material world and am open to my Higher Consciousness. I become aware of my greatness and my importance within the universe. I no longer feel inferior. I believe in myself and I believe in life. I accept myself and I love myself completely. My mission is important and I live it fully.

What I had learned from Leela was how to set boundaries and believe in myself. I still had a lot of forgiving to do with myself, and some of my vocabulary was changing, too. I was no longer blaming Joe for everything wrong in my life. I was even starting to take some responsibility for my decisions and choices. Could I have had some responsibility in contracting HIV ?

I was learning that even if I have even 1% responsibility in any of my choices and decisions, I needed to own it, in order to grow and get that weight off my back.

The Swami group, one day, was talking about this very subject. We learned that partners we have had in the past or present, that we have shared sexually with, have a part of our soul, our essence, and we need to retrieve this to become whole. Forgiveness is the key, yourself and others.

Swami was talking about those who had passed on and how you need to go to a different plane or awareness, of being, usually through meditation, and with someone who knows what they are doing to make sure you are safe in your journey. He talked about opening up a portal to travel in, and in doing so there may be other negative energy present that may try to attach itself to you, so he stressed having someone meditate with you. Like having someone with you in the shadows watching your back.

This was called soul retrieval, and after our meeting I spent time talking to him about Joe and that he was dead and I needed to find him to ask him to forgive me and retrieve my soul piece from him.

For the first time in my life, that I can remember, the word forgiveness was coming into my thoughts and more importantly, in my heart.

"Will you help me, Swami?" I asked with tears in my throat and my eyes. I knew I had to do this. I knew I had to ask Joe to forgive me for my part in our relationship that brought harm upon him, that blamed him for everything wrong and horrible in our relationship. I, for the first time in my life, was finally going to take responsibility for my choices and decisions, and I was not going to blame them on others! Poor Little Susie was finally coming to a close! I needed to ask Joe to forgive me? Wow! Now there was a new concept.

Because with this change in my heart, came the forgiveness of myself. So deeply inbedded within me, that when it finally became aware of it, it felt like someone had just punched me in the stomach. "Swami, Joe is dead, how can I ask him to forgive me, and let him know that I forgive him?" I had said with tears stuck in my throat, just a whisper of a voice.

Swami gave me a book on soul retrieval to take home and read, and said that when we met up in two weeks, we would discuss our meditation journey.

"But I want you to read this first," Swami said with a beautiful twinkle in his eyes. "Here is my phone number if you have any questions," he said.

I finished the book several days later, and Les and I talked about how I felt it applied to my life. Les agreed that this sounded like something I needed to experience with Swami to help guide me. Les had told me that he had done this a few years earlier and that he was able to clear some old karma from his life and work on his spirituality. He helped me to see things in a different light, through the light of love, not only for the rest of my soul journey, but also for others whom I may have harmed along the way.

My biggest sorrow was the fact that I had blamed Joe for everything. All my choices and decisions that caused harm to me were put on Joe's back—how I chose to deal with my HIV infection, and when I ended our relationship, also the pain and suffering I must have put Joe through while I was validating my infection caused by him and him alone. With this soul retrieval, I was finally going to take responsibility for my whole life, and knowing that without the choices and decisions that I made, I would not be able to go on and find the power of acceptance and forgiveness. There was a huge glow of a silver lining.

I would no longer say that I was knowingly infected with the HIV virus by my ex-boyfriend. While that was true, it still validated me as a victim and that I didn't need to take responsibility because it wasn't my fault. Well, that wasn't true, and it took me about ten years to come to that conclusion.

I was responsible! It wasn't long after that that my "light bulb" moment became a reality and I understood that in order to continue to grow I needed to do this and do it as soon as possible. I would be seeing Swami in nine days and I would tell him then. This was going to be some heavy meditation and I would go where I never have been before. At least, not that I remember.

A few days later, I woke up from a really strange night, and I couldn' believe what I remembered from a dream that I had. It was more than a dream, I remembered everything, every detail, how I felt and still feel. It was as if it was real. I had to run this by Les, he would know what this was. I also felt like I was a little high, and not from drugs, but from life from this vision I had awakened with.

Les told me that I had gone on my own soul retrieval and that I was probably not alone. "What? Are you kidding?" I had said, but with a knowing that this was true. And I felt like I was walking on 'cloud nine'. Ha, and now I knew what that expression meant!

The following Sunday I was ready to tell Swami what had happened. I was the first one there and I came in and said, "Swami, you are not going to believe what happened to me!" He just laughed with that little giggle he has and said, "Oh, I know because I was with you. I was behind you all the way to make sure you were safe. You did very well."

No way! I thought. Then, as if he was reading my mind, he went on to tell me what had happened. He even told me what the atmosphere was like and what Joe was even wearing. What the table and chairs were like. Well! There is something very special about this man, and I had just received a huge validation of exactly that. Hmmmmm . . . .

I call it the ethers, where I went to meet Joe. I felt that I had floated in a space and ended up in a room filled with light. There was a whiteness about it, and then I saw a table and two chairs. As I made my way to the table, I saw Joe approach, and he had a smile on his face. Funny thing was, so did I! I had no fear of Joe at all, and he looked really good.

As we sat down, we held each other's hands. This was certainly strange, I thought. We talked for what seemed like a long time. I remember asking Joe for forgiveness, and then he held out his hand like there was something in it that he wanted to give to me. IT WAS MY SOUL PIECE! I was so happy. But that wasn't all. I saw my own hand reaching out towards Joe and giving him his soul piece that I had! I remember standing up and we hugged each other and I saw Joe leave, and then so did I.

This was not going to be the last or only time I would be in the ethers, but this was an experience that I will never forget, and putting it in words now doesn't do it justice, but it still feels really good.

Chapter 42

Living in Sprague River, Oregon, in 2004 was the first time I had ever lived in the country, We were about fifty miles northeast of Klamath Falls. When we made plans to go to town, we made sure we had lists of things to get as well as all the different stops we were going to make. So when I had a doctor's appointment I always made sure, at least most of the time, that I had other things to do while in town.

I had been feeling some strangeness in my right leg. I was getting tired, and it kind of felt like shin-splints, and it also felt cold. The doctor did several tests and found I did indeed have a blockage in my leg and I needed surgery to replace the blockage with a synthetic tubing in order to clear the obstruction. This was known as

PAD (peripheral artery disease).The doctor who did my surgery said that this is usually seen in older people, so we will just put this little disease into the AIDs file.

I came through surgery just fine and was home in about five days, but because this was my right leg I wasn't be able to drive for a few weeks. It was at this time that I started making my own cards. Out here in Sprague River I joined the Homemakers Club, as well as Friends of the Library. I also had many friends stop by to see how I was doing and some of them brought me some very delicious meals. Through the Homemakers Club not only did I learn to make cards, but I also started sewing.

I had plenty of time to do all of these things, and when I was finally healed up from surgery I was able to drive to my club meetings. I called this my playtime. With the cards I made, we were able to sell them in the little local restaurant, and the monies went for community needs in our town.

We were having a sew day in town one day, and as I was driving into town, I started to feel a pain in my left arm, and my neck was hurting. By the time I got to town, Sprague River, and told the girls what was going on, they made me go over to the church where there just happened to be a rural doctor there seeing people. So I went there and told him what was happening with me, and sure enough he sent me to the hospital.

I ended up at Rogue Valley Medical Center, a hospital in Medford, Oregon, about eighty miles over the mountains from where we lived. Sure enough, I had suffered two mild heart attacks. I was going to need surgery so the doctor could put in a stent to remove the blockage.

As I was waiting in my little cubicle, the surgeon came in and introduced himself.

"Hello, Susan, my name is Dr. Kotter, and I will be doing your surgery today. Do I know you? Your name and face seem so familiar to me."

"I have never been here so I don't think so." I said with a smile.

He had a very puzzled look on his face. "You know, by law, am not supposed to ask you this, because it really makes no difference to me, so if you don't want to answer it, I will completely understand, but something is making me ask this."

I started to laugh. I had found that to be true in my own life, when you say or do something you would normally not do, but do it anyway. So I let him off the hook and said, "Go ahead Doctor, ask me anything.

"Susie how did you contract HIV?"

As I told him, his eyes got bigger and bigger and he jumped up from the side of my bed, and said, "OH MY GOD!!! I do know you! I followed your story! Both cases! I even went to hear you speak at one of your engagements! I always wondered what had happened to you. I can't believe you are here in front of me! And alive!"

Well, I was getting kind of embarrassed by all of this. And after a bit of time I was whisked off for surgery, but not before Dr. Kotter informed me that I was in good hands. Go figure, after all these years, and in a different state.

With that taken care of I got back into sewing and ended up buying a new sewing machine. I started taking some classes in Klamath Falls, and it has been the most awesome hobby for me to get into. And even here, in Payson Arizona, where I live now with my brother, Les, it has become my medication that I take to help me relive this journey and write about it for me and for you. It is my unwinding medicine, sort of like an anti-depressent.

So please, know the signs of heart attacks. They took me completely by surprise, and I didn't even know I was having them. I felt some pain and just thought it was heartburn, but it was not. I am also very thankful that there was a doctor out there in Sprague River that day who sent me to the hospital. It's amazing how things and people are there right at the perfect time, and that was just another validation that I am taken care of, that I am important, that I am protected, and that there are more lessons to learn.

Here are a couple of those affirmation cards I used to reprogram the negativity in my brain, and at the end of this book, I will include a list of books that have helped me and educated me along the way as well as a list of these cards that became one of my shining silver linings.

#1—I AM HEALTH

Each and every one of my cells is constantly regenerating itself and radiating Light. I attune myself to the divine love within me and let it flow though every single cell of my being. I breath in life and the energy flows freely within me.

#2—RELEASING

I release all grudges, all judgment, all unforgiveness. I express those things that hurt me, all those things that saddened me, all things that upset me; all that I perceive as harmful. My words allow me to release any heavy crystallization within me. As I share my feelings and learn to assert myself, I release, I regain my lightness of self.

#3—Transformation

I no longer resist life. I let myself be guided by the Light and welcome what life offers. It does not matter any more what happens, because I lift my thoughts up to my God within and I am transformed. I seek the positive in each situation and welcome what life has to teach me. I go forward trusting the path I am on.

Chapter 43

In August of 2006 I was up in Spokane, Washington, visiting my daughter, grandson, and other family and friends. I had been having trouble with my right leg again. It would become numb and cold, and then those sensations would go away. This happened several times. Finally, the day before I was leaving to go back home, I told Marie that maybe I should go over to emergency hospital and get it checked out before I headed home. She agreed with me. I told her I was going to feel really stupid if it was just due to lack of exercise, and Marie said, "Better that than something really serious, mom."

We went to Valley Hospital Emergency and after about an hour, they said they were sending me to

Sacred Heart Hospital in downtown Spokane—a very large and top-notch hospital. They were going to transfer me by ambulance, and I asked, "Why can't Marie take me?"

"We just want to make sure nothing goes wrong."

Go wrong? What are you suspecting is wrong? Oh no! I feel another bombshell coming, and I don't like it . . . .

"We think there is a blood clot that is causing a blockage in your leg," the doctor said.

I looked at Marie, "It's no big deal, honey." I had said with fake conviction in my voice. "I've been through this before."

"Well, at least they can take care of it before you leave. Good timing I think. I will meet you up there after I go pick up your grandson. You will be fine mom, see you soon." KABOOM!

I remember getting to the hospital and them transferring me to a gurney, and then lights out!

Chapter 44

I was in CCU (Critical Care Unit) at Sacred Heart Hospital for the next twelve days. I have very little memory of this time, but what I do remember is remarkable.

I find myself looking down on me, and boy oh boy, I don't look good. My color is dark and gray at the same time. There are all kinds of tubes and I.V.s around me. I see my daughter with her husband, Bob. Oh, she has turned into him crying. How sad. I see also my oldest son Donnie, and Lynn, my youngest sister is there and my brother Mick. I am leaving this scene and I am floating up, up, up.

I find myself in a room similar to the room I had met Joe in. It is light, and there are many people there, some I know, most of them I don't. I also notice for the first time there is something around my left ankle. It's a very thin ribbon of gold. For some reason I never get tangled up in it. Strange.

This is like a family reunion, I think. There is my mom and dad! They are coming over to me and we hug and talk and laugh. I see my great-grandmother, Granma Maher, I see Georgie! I hear him say, "Hi, girlfriend," and he waves that funny "queen" wave. I hear my friend, Gayle (Millie) call my nick-name," Hi Margret."

The atmosphere is calm, soft and floaty. I have no idea how long I have been there, for there was no time. No day or night, and the gold ribbon is following me where ever I go.

Then it was time for me to go, to go back to my body. I don't remember what was said or even if I was told I needed to go back. It was just time. It must have been given to me in thought. Anyway, as I turn to leave, I hear Georgie say, "You aren't going to win, if you don't buy a ticket!" Seriously! Thats what I hear and then his laugh.

I wake up in terrible pain in my leg, and the nurses aren't listening to me. They say they have me on as much pain medication as they can give me, and I tell them over and over again there is something wrong with my leg. So, for some reason I call Marie, and tell her that they aren't listening to me. I was told later that my family had been there holding vigil for many days, and had finally gone home. So twelve days later, at 2:30 AM, I finally come out of my coma and start screaming in horrible pain.

When my family arrived they insisted on getting hold of my primary doctor. Finally orders came in to take the stitches out of my leg. It turned out that I had had surgery on my leg. They had cut a five-inch gash on both sides of my leg to allow for swelling, and stitched these up, and that was what was causing this unbelievable pain. So they took the stitches out and put butterfly bandages on instead to hold the wound edges together. Well, that didn't feel very good either, and while they were doing this, they discovered that indeed the bandages were on too tight and were cutting off the flow of blood to my leg. Had they not taken the bandage and stitches out at that time I would have become septic and died in a few hours! Wow, Hu! So I figure I came back into my body at the perfect time to save my own life! Now, that is incredible!

I was sent back to my body at the right time! Who says we have control of our lives! I slowly came out of my healing. I was moved from the CCU unit to the ICU unit and then to a private room close by the nurse's station. Each move brought me closer to healing, and fewer tubes and machines. Finally a regular hospital room, yeah!

Richard and Roseanne came to see me once I was moved to a ICU unit, and told them that they were family. By then, they really were! I still looked terrible and was very sick. But my friend did what she does best, she started to do her Reiki healing on me, and Richard, always the skeptic, was forced for the first time to witness a healing. And as Roseanne pulled all this darkness out of me and swept it away, I started to change color, from a dull grayish tinge to a fleshy pink color. I slept through all of this and their visit, so to hear this from Richard, later, was a real treat.

"You should have seen it. Susie! I am now a believer! I saw this dark, gray cloud being swept out of your body, thrown down to the floor and disappear, before my very own eyes! And, and your color changing to this pink, healthy glow! WOW! It was really something!" By the time he was done with his story, I was laughing so hard, it hurt. He was so excited. Even to this day, when it comes up in conversation, we all start laughing when he retells his story with the same excitement, but now he is laughing and shaking his head. "Now that was something!"

I was very thankful I still had my foot. I was very thankful I had my leg. Now I would learn how to walk again. It would never be the same, but that's okay, I will learn to live with what I have. And I will always be on special medication just for the damage to my leg.

After several days of physical therapy, I graduated to a walker. I was always exhausted after therapy, and learned to take extra pain medication before therapy, just so I could get through It. Thank you, thank you, thank you for pain medication.

This particular day in the hospital I was able to walk down to the nurse's station with a walker! Major breakthrough! And when they saw me, they all started clapping and smiling and saying things like, "Wow, look at you," and "Way to go, Susie." One very special person, a nurses' aide, Herb, came up to me and hugged me and said, "Ah Susie, I knew you could do it!" And I was so happy. I started to cry happy tears. I couldn't wait to show Marie.

My hospital stay would end up being twenty-four days, with twelve days in a coma, floating around in the ethers. That's what I call it for me. I didn't know if it was an out-of-body experience, although I was out of my body, or was it a near-death experience? I don't know, so I call it 'the ethers'.

Talking to my family, they were able to fill in the earth time of when I was gone. They even said that there were times I was carrying on regular conversations. I have no memory of this. Strange! Hu! My family would help me fill in those blanks over the next several months. It was very difficult for Marie to tell me what she remembered because she almost lost me.

"This is really hard for me, mom, because we thought you weren't going to make it. I felt I was watching you die, and I really don't want to relive it." It took her a long time before she could talk about it.

It did help her when I told her about being in "the ethers," and helping her realize that even when we do cross over, we are still here, that there is life there, that our soul lives on, it's just the vessel, the bag of bones, that we leave behind, and no matter what happens or how we die, we are still around.

It was a few days before I was going to be released from the hospital and I was sitting in a chair in my room. It looked to be a beautiful day outside with blue sky and sunshine, and I had a nice view of Spokane out my window. I was just sitting there pondering all that had taken place in my life. Trying to make sense out of it all. Trying to find a silver lining. What was the point of all of this?

My door was open but the curtain was closed in my room. I didn't like people just looking in my room as they walked by. Suddenly I looked up and here comes my mom and dad, holding hands and smiling. Not a word was said but conversations were conducted like telepathy. And this felt like no big deal, they just came by for a visit. Remember, my mom and dad are dead, and have been for a while. We had just had a visit in the 'ethers' not too long ago.

Mom looked wonderful! She had on her favorite pink outfit and her turban. She wore them when she was going through chemotherapy, and dad looked like he always did, in a shirt and blue jeans. What was really unusual was that I noticed they were holding hands. I had never seen that when they were alive. For some reason I didn't think it odd that two dead people were walking into my hospital room, but that they were holding hands. Go figure, Hu!

They came over to where I was sitting, one on each side of me, and kissed me on the sides of my head. As they put their arms around me, their arms felt like feathers, but they looked like arms!

"Susie, we are very proud of you. You have more work to do. You will be okay. We are here for you."

And then they just left. Just the way they arrived, out through the curtain and out of my room. Now, you might be thinking, this woman is crazy!!! Ha ha. I am not. I just sat there in my chair and thought I just had a visit from my mom and dad, how cool.

I really had to ponder this for a while because it was so unusual. How was I going to explain this to people? I came up with, just tell them. It doesn't really matter what people choose to believe, because this happened to you, for you. Well, that was true. Maybe there is more to this. Maybe it happened to me to share with those who need to hear this, to help them feel 'they are not alone'. Maybe to help them put some puzzle pieces of their lives together.

I was told before I left the hospital that I was going to have to move back to Spokane in order to receive my major medical care and therapy. Here I had family, and they could help me. Being down in Sprague River, a fifty-mile drive to town, therapy at least three times a week was not going to work. But for the next six weeks I would be having home therapy at Marie and Bob's place.

I was very sad because I didn't want to move here. I didn't want to leave Les or my home. But Les worked full time. How was he going to get me to therapy? Yes, I was going to miss my friends and Swami. But I wanted to be able to walk, and I was very thankful I had my leg. Extensive therapy was my only shot! There were still no guarantee's I would have full use of my leg, but I had to try. Maybe someday I would be able to go back home. Ah, was this just me with my rose-colored glasses on, or was I working on my intention?

Even though I was counting my blessings, I was very hurt that I had to move. Why! Why! What the hell is this supposed to mean? I don't see any silver lining here! And I became very angry. I did not understand why my life had taken such a dramatic turn.

I was able to move into my old apartment building, which was a miracle in and of itself. Tony, the on site manager, had told me that this apartment must have been waiting just for me. "Susie I don't understand why this apartment had been vacant for 3 months!" He had said with a laugh. This time I was moving into a one-bedroom. It seemed so small to me. Even though there was a place available to rent, I started to cry. None of this made me happy, and as soon as I finished my therapy at Marie's home, I would have to drive home to pack up my stuff and move my life! My hopes and dreams and, most of all my best friend and brother, Les, was going to be left behind. He is going to be there all by himself. Steven was gone and now me. Was he going to be okay? Was I?

As I pulled out of the driveway in my U-Haul, heading back up to Spokane, I wasn't thinking of any full circles, or silver linings, or a new beginning. I was thinking of me and my brother, and how I didn't want to leave, and I felt I was forced to because of my health. I was not feeling "spiritual" at all! I was not embracing this new beginning! I was angry and mad and sad, and before I was even out of the driveway, I was crying, crying, crying. Have you ever tried to drive when you are crying? I even had to pull off the road several times! And here I was driving out of this fantastic life I had here with my brother, into a new one that I didn't want . . . I cried all the way to Biggs, Oregon, about 250 miles north where I stayed the night. My heart was broken. And that was going to take time to heal, as well as my leg.

Chapter 45

When I got up in the morning, I felt a little different, a little better, at least I wasn't crying. Off to Spokane. When I pulled into the parking lot of my apartment, my family and some friends were there waiting for me. It helped that they were very happy to see me, and they had me moved in within a couple of hours. It would take me at least three months to unpack. I was in no hurry.

I moped around for quite some time feeling sorry for myself. This was a big setback for me and I was not happy! I did nothing for about two and a half months except go to doctors' appointments and therapy. I had no car so it was either special transport or by family and friends. At least I was within walking distance to the library, grocery store, and a Jo-Ann's fabric store. But even that didn't bring me any joy. I felt lost. I felt my life had been pulled out from under me, and I was just going to have to accept it. I was going to have to put into practice all that I had learned from Les and Swami—find the silver lining and create a new life for myself. BUT I DON'T WANT TOO!!!!!!! I WANT MY LIFE BACK !!! I must say, I was on quite a 'pity party'!

I found that over the years it was much easier to tell people how wonderful my life had become; That I am on a wonderful spiritual path full of light and love; that full circles and silver linings are the icing on the cake—Look! Look! Look! There it is! Oh yeah, it's real easy to tell people to look beyond and within themselves when everything is wonderful in your life . . . . But when your own life that you loved is suddenly not there, when the going got tough, I crumbled! I crumbled into the old "poor little Susie" routine!

I didn't or couldn't practice what I had preached. I was in the throes of a huge self-inflicted pity—party. I called Les all the time. I missed him so much. It seemed he was getting along without me just fine; he did have his job after all. But I knew that he would come home to an empty and cold home since we heated with wood and had a great Earth stove, and no cooked meals or desserts to smell or rummage through the fridge for something good to eat. But most of all he would be coming home to a silent and empty home, and that was not good. So I knew deep down inside that he was probably not doing so well either, but he would do a lot better than me. Les never wallowed in pity, he just went on . . . .

December 25, 2006.KABOOM !!!

I was out at my younger sister's house for the holidays. There were her friends from work that would be there, my brother Mick, Marie and her family, and my son Donnie. He was out of prison and this was our first Christmas together in years. This should have been one fantastic and happy time for all of us. But it wasn't. There was lots of booze, lots of drugs, and I was disgusted by the whole thing, but I had no way to leave. I felt trapped. So I just stayed in the living room most of the time with a few people watching a game on TV. Then the phone rang and it was for me. Who would be calling me here? It was Les, and he called to say he thought he was having a heart attack and wanted to say goodbye to me!

"No, I am not going to the hospital, if it's my time then I will go. I am asking you, Susie, to just let me go this way, but I needed to call and tell you."

What??? Oh MY GOD! NO, NO, NO! PLEASE DON'T GO !!!! Don't do this Les!

When I finally got off the phone with my best friend, I was in a bucket of tears. I really didn't know what to do. I couldn't leave and drive down to Sprague River, 600 miles away, in the winter with snow and ice on the roads. I felt that this was the last straw!

On my third call to Les, I was finally able to say to him, "Do you want to end up paralyzed in a wheelchair? Needing help to go to the bathroom? Someone to feed you? You just might not die! Have you thought about that?"

"Well, I am feeling a little better, maybe it was just heartburn, but I have to get ready to go to work, so I will talk to you later." He said it like it was no big deal!

Oh, he could be so stubborn at times. And to go to work? When just a few hours before he thought he was dying?

Les worked at the casino, so it wasn't like it was the most important job in the world. I felt, if anything, he should at least stay home, but, Oh no, not my brother! Then I thought, what if he has an accident on his way to work? Well, I will call when he is supposed to be on duty, just to make sure he got there. God!!!I hated not being there, and stuck here!

When he got to work, everyone there told him to go to the hospital. They wanted to call an ambulance but instead he chose to drive. But at least he had agreed to go. When he called me back around 9 PM he was to stay overnight there. It was a stroke, high blood pressure. But thank his lucky stars, no lasting effects.

"Susie, I want to thank you for keeping your promise to let me do this my way. I know it was asking a lot that you didn't call everyone, so thanks for keeping your word. I will be fine now."

If I had been there I would have probably "crossed him over" myself! I had felt so helpless, but I guess, I was meant to be on the sidelines.

Chapter 46

In February of 2007, I found myself in the doctor's office, asking for help with my depression. And I was very depressed. I had to find me. I had lost me. I was going to go see my best friend, Fez, Les, Bro, whichever name I called him by. I had to go see him and I would leave towards the end of April. My biggest fear was that I would be worse when I came back, because I would be leaving again.

I remember telling the psychologist, "You have three months to heal me. I don't want this drawn out into months and years! I want you to help me find my path. I will work very hard to heal, and you need to give me things to work on. I need to be given goals to reach and whatever will help me find my silver lining, my joy. If it is to be a new life, then help me find a way to accept it. Help me find something I will want to come back to once I go visit my Les." I said it with as much passion I could muster.

It was at this time that I had been led to reach out to my sister Julia. We had become estranged after my court case way back when. I remember that that was one of the things I had left the ethers with. I needed to get in touch with Julia.

I had been putting it off ever since I had moved back to Spokane. And now this message was invading my dreams and thoughts. I was afraid that Julia wouldn't want to have anything to do with me. I had felt I had let Julia down. That I should have gotten punitive monies in my case, and because I hadn't, I had disappointed her, and all the "dirty little things" with my relationship with Joe, she now knew about. Well, I was just so ashamed about all the things that went on behind closed bedroom doors, I couldn't face her. Wow! I was still carrying that around with me? I thought I had dealt with that way back then, too! Guess not.

I finally called, and kept thinking, oh please, please don't reject me. I told Julia that I was living back in Spokane, and would she like to come over for lunch and get reacquainted? I don't know how long I held my breath until she said YES !!! Oh my, now what.

We had a simple lunch of tomato soup and grilled cheese sandwiches. Then Julia starting talking. It just seemed she needed to get a lot of things off her chest. A lot of hurts and pain and assumptions. For some reason I just let her talk. She talked about how everyone had put her up on a pedestal and she could not live up to what people thought she should be or do. This was a very heavy burden to carry around for such a long time, and I felt that with just the purging all of this muck from her life, and from mine, we would be able to start a rediscovery of our sisterhood.

Throughout the next couple of months we started to share many things about each other. We told funny things about our childhood as well as very painful ones. How we both learned very early in life to walk on broken glass. Our dad was very violent when he was drinking, and we also learned to stay out of site. Our mom and little brother got most of dads wrath.

We talked about my medical stuff as well as Julia's. She had diabetes that she managed. I had HIV that I managed. But still my biggest concern was my foot and leg, and managing peripheral artery disease, PAD.

I still wasn't sewing very much, and I wasn't really making my cards, but I was sure reading a lot. I was finding my way back to my spiritual path in the different books I was getting from the library. I was walking a lot and the walk up to the Library was about one and a half miles round trip, and up and down hills. A good workout for me. And I started to find beauty and joy in my daily walks around my neighborhood. It was a very beautiful neighborhood, with all kinds of trees and flowers every where. Small changes were starting to take shape, my attitude was slowly changing.

I saw Richard and Roseann often. I would just hang out with them. They were always telling me how good I looked and that I was really getting around better. There encouragement really fed my healing, and with Roseann being a Reiki Master, well, let's just say I was in really good hands.

My walking was getting better. My foot was still an issue as far as the pain, but I was either getting used to it or it wasn't as bad. And I reminded myself every day of that very important fact! I had my big sister in my life, and that was a big bonus. Hey! Could this be another full circle? Could this be a silver lining? Could this be the reason I needed to move back to Spokane in the first place?

I would be spending a month with my special friend in a few weeks. So yeah! Things were better than they were a month ago, two months ago. That's how I needed to focus, for that damn silver lining was out there and I was very determined to find it. Or had I already?

The other bright spot in my life was my daughter, Marie. I saw her as much as I could. But she was a working girl, with her own family, and there were times I couldn't understand why she always had to ask her husband, Bob, if I could come over. But that was just the way it was. She and my grandson, Jay, did come over to my place often, but only for short periods of time.

My mental health doctor and I were working on setting up things for me to do, that I could do when I got back from seeing Les. Something I could look forward to so it wouldn't hurt so bad leaving him when the time came to come back. They weren't big things, but at least they were something. Julia and I would start sewing together. She is what I call, for me, a master quilter. She can sew and make anything! Really. She even made her daughter's wedding dress, something I find so fascinating, even to this day.

I was also going to take lots of pictures while I was with Les, then come home and scrapbook them for Les' birthday gift. These things would help make the trip home easier, and most of all, I was going to step up the therapy on my leg and push even harder to become even more mobile. The last time Les saw me, I couldn't even move my toes. So some progress had been made; now I could move a couple of them a little bit.

Chapter 47

About two weeks before I left for Sprague River, (I was going by train, which is a really fun way to travel, that is, if you have the time) my grandson, Jay, was spending a few hours with me when the intercom to my apartment buzzed.

"Hey, Nana, it's Aunt Julia," Jay shouted. I remember laughing because you could whisper and be heard, that's how small my apartment was.

"Come on up, Julia." I had said.

"No, no, you have to come down to the parking lot, see this cute little car we just bought." Julia said with a lot of excitement. I knew that Ryan and Julia had been looking for a little car for her to do her running around in, instead of their big truck. So down the stairs and out the door Jay and I went.

There was Julia standing by a cute little Chevy station wagon, chocolate brown and the interior in perfect condition. It needed a paint job but besides that it was perfect. It seemed that it was a one-owner car. The person used it to go back and forth to work in and that was all! For being over 20 years old, it was excellent.

"Wow, Julia," I said, "This is just perfect for you."

And she said, "So, you like it?" with a big grin on her face.

"Yeah, what's not to like," I said, laughing.

"Oh I am so glad," she said, and then she had told me to hold out my hand, and dropped the keys to this cute chocolate brown Chevy wagon in it and said, "That's good because we bought it for you, something to come back to."

I just looked at my sister and I did what I do best, I burst out in tears. We grew up naming cars. Why? I think it was because to have one was a really big deal for us. So they were important enough to name. We also grew up with dad wrecking many of them because of his drinking.

In the few months that we had come back into each other's lives, and for Julia and Ryan to do something like this for me, I just couldn't believe it. It was the best thing to come back to. Now I just had to learn to drive with no feeling in my foot. We all collectively named the car, Hershey, because it looked like a Hershey chocolate bar, and I love chocolate! No, really, I love it, to the point of an addiction. I will make myself sick on it.

When I get back from seeing Les, I thought, I will have a freedom I have not had before, this time around in Spokane. It's really amazing how it feels to have something like your own wheels, and how we have a way of taking that for granted. Only when it became something that was taken from my life and then given back, could I appreciate such a gift. Now Julia and I could sew together, run around in my new car, and just do things that sisters do together.

It brought back a memory of my mom. One day my mom and Marie were at the store getting groceries. When they were finished and got into the car to leave, mom couldn't get her car to start. (her car's name was 'good girl') She tried over and over again and nothing. She called my dad at work to come and get them and when he got there the car started up right away. This was quite confusing, but the car went into the shop anyway. In a few days the car was returned home.

One day very soon after this incident my mom shared with me what happened. We were sitting out on their deck having some ice tea. Nice and warm summer day.

"Susie, I am going to sell Good Girl."

"Why, mom, what's going on?" I said with shock in my voice. And then she had told me.

"Do you remember a few days ago when the car broke down at the store, and your dad had to come and get us? It seems that I had had a blockage of memory. There wasn't anything wrong with the car, Susie. It was me. What if someday I forget how to stop the car? And what if I had my granddaughter with me like the other day? I could hurt someone else. So it's time to give it up, honey. The cancer is back, and it is invading my brain."

Ah, mommy, I remember that conversation like it was yesterday, and we both had sat on the bench outside on the deck and cried. That was in September of 1991, and she passed in March of 1992. Not only had my mom lost the freedom of travel—I also had experienced that.

Freedom of having a car was and is the best! The gift that Ryan and Julia had just given me was a real turning point in my life and I am sure they both acquired jewels in their crowns, yeah!

Chapter 48

Ah, this feels so good, I remember saying to myself as the train pulled into the station in Klamath Falls around 9 PM. I saw Les in the crowd waiting for me. With tears in my eyes we hugged and laughed and hug some more. By the time we got home it was around 10:30. I was exhausted and went straight to bed, but not before I looked around the house and saw all the things my brother had done through the winter.

I woke up the next morning to the smell of coffee, and went out to the sunroom with my coffee to see my bro. Oh, it felt so good to be back, even if it was just a visit. We talked a lot about my recovery, and had I been working on healing myself? I told him about the walks and the therapy I was still in, and showed him my progress, like finally moving my toes. "And did you notice I am walking without a walker, or cane?" I was so excited to be able to show him this!

"That's not what I am talking about, Susie. Are you working mentally on your leg, foot, and toes, to heal? Are you doing that? You have the power to heal all of this, you know. But you have to want it! Remember DESIRE, BELIEVE, and INTENT! Are you doing that?"

Oh MY God! No, I have not been doing that! It had not even crossed my brain! Now that was a bombshell! Talk about living your truth! And I forgot the most important lesson I had learned all these years—Physician, heal thyself!

I had already made HIV a non-issue in my life; that is to say, it was not my focus on my life, it no longer defined who I was. This I could manage, just like Julia had with her diabetes. But my leg and the PAD was a major issue. Les did Reiki healing on my leg, and by the time I had to return home I did indeed feel a lot better. It was he who had given me a shot of "health", and I was going to take it home with me and work! Work! Work on my leg! And as Les reminded me, I am in charge of my reality! I can write this script of my life. Yes, desire, belief, and intent. Yes, I can heal myself! Silver lining, here I come!

It felt really good to see my Swami group again, and boy, were they surprised to see me, except Swami. For some reason he always knows things, ha. Hard to sneak up on that guy. And he, too, reminded me of my self-healing and of what good friends I had here.

We also went to one of our favorite places, Mount Shasta. We couldn't get to Panther Meadows because of the snow, but that was okay, because just to gaze upon the mountain was healing in itself. And the small city of Mount Shasta was really fun to shop in. The Crystal Shop has always been one of our favorite and just the feel of the store is amazing.

I was so glad I had things to look forward to when I got home, because it was indeed hard to leave. Remember those affirmation cards I told you about? They are called Messages Of Light.

Before I left to catch the train to go back to Spokane, I pulled out one of the cards and this is the one I pulled.

The title was *My Inner Calling . . . .*" I now see that all situations in my life that cause resentment are ideal opportunities to work on my inner self. These ordeals are necessary for my growth as I become aware of my dualities. Thus I de-dramatize situations and have access to positive cause of my experience. . . .

Oh My God! Was that ever a slap in the face for me, and Les and I laughed about it all the way to the station. If those cards didn't force me to find a silver lining to living in Spokane and not here with my brother, then what would?

Swami had reminded me that I was the master of my life, and I was the one to rise above my doubts, to believe in myself, and that life lessons are just another "growing" time.

"Look Susie, for the silver lining is right in front of you!" My higher self, that voice within me, was shouting . . . . Yes, indeed.

Chapter 49

Julia picked me up at the train station at 12:30 in the morning, and it was a very wonderful thing to do for anyone! While I was waiting for her, a girl who asked me if I had any change I could spare so she could get something to eat. Now, I think that at one time or another we have all been approached by others—can you spare a dime, sir? I didn't have any money but I did have some leftover food she could have. Her face lit up and she said, "Oh yeah, lady, that would be great!" And she sat down beside me and ate everything I had! I also ended up giving her my coat. It was cold out, and I had more coats at home.

This incident reminded of my grandma, feeding that "bum" who came to her door. When I had asked her why she had done that, her reply was, "Well Susie, you never know when that might be Jesus in disguise . . . ."

WOW! What a full circle that was, and I had forgotten all about it. I guess that comes in having a past to look upon. Others may call it wisdom, I just call it, Wow! And I still smile when I think of that moment and wonder how that person is today. I send love every time it crosses my mind. You can, too. I also find that when you send love to those hurtful and painful parts of your life, it for some reason doesn't have the sting that it had before. Try it and see for yourself. In that quiet place in your soul. See how good it feels to do that and the more you do it, the better you feel! For me it's like my own little soul energy boost.

For the next several months I threw myself into my therapy and my walks, and stopped going to my mental health doctor for depression therapy. I was really feeling so much better and I was getting around so much better with my little car.

I was also doing my healing meditation at least twice a day, when I got up in the morning and when

I went to bed. And now that I had wheels I was able to go over to Richard and Roseanne's place or over to Marie's or over to Julia's. What a difference a car makes, ha.

One day while I was at my HIV doctor's appointment, he asked me if I would consider going to an HIV group that was starting. They would deal with a different subject each week, and with my experience I would be quite an asset for all the others who were newly infected, or just dealing with it for the first time in their lives. They may have been infected for years, but just recently, reaching out for help. "And with your background, you could really help a lot of people who have committed to participate in this group!" My doctor pleaded with me. I told him I needed time to think about it, and that I would get back to him. This group was really going to be deep, and might open up some old wounds that I had, and I really didn't want to go down that path . . . . oops, that sounded a lot like me, me, me.

I ran this by my very intuitive special friend, Roseanne.

Susie Wyatt-Clemens

"SUSIE !! You were meant to do this! You have to do this. You have to help them. You and you alone may be the only person that can help them! YOU HAVE TO DO THIS ! This may be why this happened to you, did you stop and think of that? This may be that 'silver lining' you keep talking about! DO IT,DO IT, DO IT!

Well, I really was not expecting that kind of reaction, and I was shocked at how serious she was in slapping me into shape. This wasn't about me, me, me. I kind of went home with my tail between my legs and sat there, pondering my smack-down. I thought I would get a second opinion, so I called my very dear friend Linda. We had been in the WABA (Women Affected By AIDS) group in the mid-90's. She moved to western Washington, and we stayed in touch where ever either of us moved to. Plus she also was infected by her boyfriend, but unlike me, she stayed with him until he died. Linda has been 'that angel' in my life. The one person in my life that has always been there for me, no matter what. We never had to explain things. We just had a knowingness about each other.

After I explained the situation to her, she also informed me that I really needed to do this for them!

"You don't have any idea, Susie, how just having you as my friend, someone I could lean on in those early years really helped me. And the strength to go through those law cases, for all of us. You showed us all how to be a survivor. Have you forgotten? Yes, yes you need to do this!"

And she said this with such conviction, oh boy, I guess I should. Bummer! I wanted all of this behind me, but maybe this could be the last of it. Yeah, that was it! I needed to do this once and for all, there must be some unfinished business I need to do, to take care of.

I then remembered something I could teach them—something that gave me the strength to go on, and that was "Being a victim limits you in fear. Being a survivor gives you the strength to change the world!" Yes, that's it! My friend, Gayle. I remembered when she gave me that little tid-bit years ago, when I was sitting in the waiting room of the Prosecuting Attorney's office, getting ready to give my deposition to Joe's attorney. The one little sentence that changed my life!

I could also share with them the Messages of Light cards, which helped me find the love of self I needed so desperately. Instead of the guilt and anger for myself and the negative emotions I carried, such as, "You deserve this, You are no good, What did you expect, This is all your fault." Man, I didn't need to be so harsh on myself. Maybe they feel that way also, and maybe they have infected others. Now that would be very hard to live with.

I was already thinking of things I could do as I made the phone call to commit to this group, this six-week course. It was to start the following Wednesday.

Chapter 50

There were twenty-four of us at the group meeting. Some were very shy, some were very vocal. Some were laughing while some seemed very sad. Some were in their twenties while most were thirties and forties. Two of us were in our fifties.

We were asked to go around the room and introduce ourselves and tell a little bit about ourselves. After we had done that, Doug, the head of the group, asked me if I would share my story with this group. It had been at least ten years earlier when I had given my last speaking engagement, and it really felt different now. Here was a group of HIV/AIDS-infected people in front of me, and I felt some apprehension! That was very strange, at least for me. I had always felt very comfortable in front of an audience, so what was different?

After I had finished, one of the women was really crying. I went up to her, and put my arms around her, and in an instant we both knew who we were. The rest of the group were totally silent . . . . through her tears she said, "You! You were Joe's girlfriend! I'm, I'm Amber, Joe's girl-friend, before he went to Prison!"

HOLY SHIT!!!!!! Who would have ever thought we would meet, for the first time, fourteen years later in a special support group, in Spokane Washington; that I would be face to face with the Amber we had searched for all those years earlier! And here she was, face to face. Wow! Talk about a full circle. Oh My . . . I was speechless.

We were moved to a room for just the two of us, and Jody who was a therapist, came with us to help mediate this meeting. My doctor was really the only one who realized what just had happened

Amber had found out she could possibly be infected with HIV from the front page of the Seattle

Times newspaper, when my story ran about Joe's arrest and what he was charged with. She had been living with her husband and two children, and had been clean and sober from heroin for over five years, and had moved to the Seattle area to start a new life. That is, until she read in the paper that we were looking for her.

She ended up in Hawaii, without her children, and stayed with the needle for a lot of years. She had returned to Spokane for an in-house substance abuse program for six months. She had only been out and starting a new life for a very few months, and here she was. Wow! It was amazing all the things that had to take place in both of our lives to make this meeting with Amber and myself a reality.

I was totally dumbfounded by this. Could this be why I am here in Spokane? To put a close on this chapter in both of our lives? Is this the reason I was supposed to be at this group meeting?

That night I had dinner at Richard and Roseanne's, and they were just as shocked as I was. We talked a lot about our paths in life and whether we really do have any control! Is this all pre-planned? I would like to think that I have had some choices of my own, but then again, maybe I was the one who went off-path, and it took a long time to get back "on the right track". Well, this kind of thinking was just going to go around and around!

After the second group meeting, I told Doug that I wouldn't be returning. It seemed that Amber wanted to attach herself to me, and I just couldn't go there. He agreed with me and said that just my telling my story to the group and what happened afterwards, had been a real eye-opener, not only for him but for the group.

Chapter 51

It had been several months now and I was making plans to go back down to see Les. I had really stepped up my therapy and one day in late July, my vascular doctor had gone through all my latest tests and was extremely pleased with my progress.

"Well, Susie, I must tell you that we all are surprised by your recovery, and would have never expected you to have come so far," she said with a big grin on her face. But it was not as big as mine! "Does this mean I can move back home?" I asked with as much hope and excitement I could only dare to have.

She looked at me and said, "Only if you promise me that you will follow up with a qualified vascular doctor!"

I hugged her, and was crying. I would have promised her anything! But yes, I could do that. Wow! Wait until Les hears this!

Because I wanted this so bad, others were excited for me also. That is, except Marie. She was okay with it but not excited. I would not understand this for about a month, when I would be coming back to Spokane from my visit with Les to pack up and move back home. Ah, that had a really good ring to it.

When Les picked me up at the train station that night, I didn't say anything to him about moving back. Instead I told him what the doctors had said and then asked him, "So do you think I can move back?" YES, YES, YES! Man, I don't know what I would have done if he had said, no!

Since it was August of 2007, we did what we like to do and that was to go camping. Les had found a really cool place in the Gearhart National Forest, about fifty miles from where we were, nice and so close. We also loved to walk up and down rivers. I didn't know how well I was going to do in the cold water, considering my foot, but I had to try. I must say I did pretty well, but I couldn't do it for very long before my foot would go numb. But it was sure fun, and to think this time I could go back to Spokane to move, well, that was all the incentive I needed.

I started to gather up boxes the day after I got back. I gave my notice to move, and ordered my U-Haul. But this time, it had a car tow. I lined up the people I would need to help pack the truck and then, Kaboom! I guess things were just going too good. But this time I didn't react like I used to. I wasn't going to butt my nose into someone else's life. But when it's your own beautiful daughter? Yes, even then.

My mom was my best friend, but in being that she would have a tendency to take over my life, which I let her do, and solve my problems for me. So, when I started to have all kinds of problems after she passed, I didn't know what to do. I wasn't taught good coping skills and how to make good solid choices. If I stayed here for Marie to help her in this very bleak choice in leaving her husband, would I be doing to her what my mom did to and for me?

One day Marie told me what it was like living with Bob. He was very verbally abusive. And then she told me he had been doing meth. And he would find something she did or didn't do and just rant and scream at her for hours.

"I didn't dare do anything to upset him, mom." And then she showed me what he did, and how he would be in her face and say things to belittle her over and over again. "Then one day we were all wrestling on the floor and Jay had nailed his dad in the balls by accident, and Bob kicked Jay so hard, mom, he flew out of control at his own son! God, mom, I thought he was going to kill him, really! That was the day I decided to leave, and Jay said yes, so while you were gone, we moved in with my dad."

Oh Missy, I am so sorry for you. This is a hard road to take, but at least you are free of this horrible abusive, drugged-out piece of . . . . Well, you get the picture. And it would be hard, and she would be finding her own silver linings—at least I taught her that. Marie would go on and find a man to share her life with and have two more grandbabies.

Chapter 52

It's funny, when I had moved up to Spokane it was in October 2006, and now I was moving back home in Sprague River Oregon, in October 2007. Everything had come full circle, and what was the reason for having to move from here for a year? Was it to finally find Amber, and put closure on that chapter in my life? Or was it something more powerful than that? Could it have been what I had left the ethers with—that knowledge, that message, to reach out and connect with my sister, Julia? Looking back on that time I would come to believe that was #1, then #2, and the third one was for Les and me to realize we were going to go through the next step of our lives with each other as brother and sister, happy as clams! So how can you tell when a clam is happy? Surprise! I don't have the answer to that, but we were sure happy.

Les and I decided in the spring that we wanted to move. He was tired of all the drama at work, and I wasn't connecting with my fair-weather friends in Sprague. But a new fabric store had opened up in Klamath Falls, that my brother found, and that was my new hangout. I began to take classes and found the love of my life! The Quilted Rooster! And the friends I met there became a real lifeline for me, and even though we were fifty miles out of town, it was worth it.

The selling of our home would be difficult but it was what we wanted to do. We fixed the place up, gave it a new face-lift, painted the sheds and the chicken coop, got the green house up and running, and de-cluttered the house. It looked great. We even installed a new shower. But we were going to use the old shower door if I could clean it up to look good as new. While Les was working inside, I was working outside. After a while I realized my right foot was going numb, Oh no! Not again! No way! Ah, Yes Way! The next day I was in the doctor's office, they were running tests, and they said, "Ah Houston, we have a problem". This time I took the ambulance over the mountains to Rogue Valley Medical Center to my top—notch vascular doctor.

"Susie, we are going to take out that synthetic tubing they put in the first time you had issues with the blockages in your leg, and use one of your own veins, which they should have done in the first place. That should take care of the problem. Oh, by the way, you caught this one really early, way to go!" He said with a smile. I had one on my face, too! I was home in a week! A very good turnaround time, ha.

Les and I spent a lot of time on the Oregon Coast, from Brookings to Port Oxford, looking for a place we wanted to live in, and decided on or around Brookings. We looked and looked and there just didn't seem to be anything that we could afford in our budget. But it didn't matter because we weren't getting any bites on the house in Sprague River. By then we were coming into the winter and decided to take the house off the market and start again next spring.

In the spring of 2009 we listed with a realtor that specialized in homes in rural areas. We de-cluttered again, and started to look again on the coast for a place to either buy or rent. Nothing! We couldn't find anything. We had a couple that seemed really interested in our place in Sprague, but nothing for sure.

Then one day while Richard and Roseanne were down visiting, a couple from southern California came by to look at the place, and I just had a feeling that they were the ones.

The last time we were on the Oregon Coast was September of 2009. We had a wonderful vacation and went camping at Humbug Camp grounds right on the ocean, and then we spent some time camping in the redwoods. And that was the most beautiful and awesome camping trip we had ever had. But something was missing and neither one of us could put our finger on it.

The night we got home we heard on the news that there had been a tsunami warning for the coast! Right where we had been! We didn't find out the details about it until the next morning, and we both looked at each other and agreed that was a sign.

"Fez, I think that was not a shot across the bow but a direct hit!"

And he said, "Susie I really think we need to look at Arizona!"

I had said for all my life as long as I can remember that Arizona was the last state I would ever move to . . . TOO HOT!

"I promise you, Susie, there really are mountains and water! Let's look into it"

It's funny how we both agreed that we really didn't want to live on the coast. It was mostly damp, rainy, sandy, windy. We both had already lived through that before on the Washington coast, and really didn't want to live like that again. What's really strange is, that as soon as we switched directions, we both woke up one morning and we had had the same dream! Really!

Chapter 53

"Fez, I had a dream last night I think we should talk about."

"Me too, Susie! But you go first."

"Well, we had moved to a place in Arizona that started with a P. It looked like it was in the mountains, and it was by water! Do they really have mountains there? Like we have here?"

Les began to laugh, and said, "I think they (meaning our guides, some people call them angels) sent us the same dream!" We started to laugh because this wasn't the first time that had happened to us, and we knew it wouldn't be the last.

I went in to the library in Klamath Falls and got a bunch of information on Arizona, some DVDs, and some travel books. The next day while we were in the sunroom having our coffee, Les said that some people at the casino where he worked had told him to check out a place called Payson.

Well, it had met the first test, it started with a P. It was near water, and looked to be in the mountains. I called the Chamber of Commerce and had them send us a packet of information and a current newspaper.

By the next weekend we got a call from our realtor. We had an offer on the house!!! Just like that! No sooner had we switched directions as far as relocating, our house sold! It was like a domino-effect. As soon as we were on the right path, we were ready. And talk about a huge leap of faith.

By December 18th, 2009, we were on our way to Payson, Arizona, with the biggest U-Haul we could get, towing our Jeep with me driving our truck, towing our travel trailer. We had bought a pair of walkie-talkies so we could talk to each other. We were so excited, like a couple of kids going to Disney—land!!!

My family and friends were shocked that I was going to Arizona! And to top it off, to a place neither one of us had ever been! Sight unseen! We just told them that, why not! We were free, and living outside the box! But actually, we were guided the whole way. This was where we were meant to be.

We pulled into Payson, Arizona, December 22, 2009 with snow at our backs, and we both were hooting and hollering, "WE MADE IT! WE ARE HERE!" We knew we were home when the first store we saw was Home Depot.

"Oh my gosh! Did you see the QUILTING SHOP !!! Well, that did it for me.

We pulled into the Comfort Inn just as the snow—yes, I said snow, started to fall. By the time we got into our room, the flakes were as big as silver dollars, and we collapsed on our beds and laughed, and laughed.

"Hey! Wasn't this what we moved away from?" We both said.

When I had called the Chamber of Commerce for the packet of information, I had asked them about the snow because we would be at an elevation of around 5000 feet, the same elevation we had in Sprague River, but in Oregon we were just on the east side of the Cascade Mountain Range.

"Well, honey, we do get snow, about a couple of times throughout the winter, but we call it 'designer snow'. That's when you run outside and take a picture because in a few hours it will be gone!" And she laughed. And now we were, too. Kind of like the guides telling us, "You are home, enjoy!"

We rented a place out about six miles from town called Beaver Valley Estates, right on the East Verdi River, and six months later Les bought a wonderful log home out here!

"Well, don't you remember what you told me years ago?" Sharon, my trucker friend from Spokane said when I called her.

"No, give me a hint?" I said through my laughs.

"Well, you told me one time that your dream one day would be to live by a river, in a log home. Guess you were right, but I doubt you thought it would be in Arizona! Hu!" and we both laughed and laughed.

Now that's a full circle!

Chapter 54

Now, tell me, who wouldn't go to a retreat in Sedona????

It was a retreat for people with HIV/AIDS, and caregivers. It would be just for the weekend, full of the most recent information and an opportunity, my case manager here had told me, to meet others around the area, especially women.

"Wow, Susie! You have to go, please! Your story, and what you not only have gone through, what you can teach all of us, but how you got through all of it!" Mel said with such excitement in her voice. How could I say no.

I wondered what it was going to be like, to walk through those doors of the retreat. I was reminded of my first retreat in 1993, at the Bozarth Center in Spokane Washington, The Strength For The Journey retreat.

Here I am, seventeen years later, getting ready to go to my first HIV/AIDS retreat in Arizona, not as a severely wounded, devastated woman, but as a woman who beat the odds of my life ending at fifty years of age. A woman who in 1993, saw the worst of what this heinous disease could do to people, and what humankind could and did do, to people. As they say, THE GOOD, THE BAD, THE UGLY!

Would I find progress? Would I find hope? What kind of misconceptions would we still be battling? What kind of half-truths, and prejudices would still be out there? I must say that at least I didn't find the shocking display of illness and "the walking dead," that was present at my first retreat. Or was that because this time I was ready to see the worst this disease had to offer? Either way, when I walked into the reception room, I was met with laughter, music, and a feeling of happiness! Wow, what a difference!

Throughout the weekend I had found that some things hadn't changed, and one of them was the way people were still contracting this disease—through unsafe sex. Many of the women were infected the way I had been, but had no voice, were still angry, and didn't really tell others, except family members and close friends. They had no avenue to heal, except for small intimate, groups that might meet once a month, if they were lucky.

The biggest concern for most of us was health care! There was a time when we couldn't or wouldn't take our antiretroviral meds because they made us so sick. Now, we know that is what is giving us a fighting chance, the opportunity to manage this ugly and painful dis-ease.

This dis-ease no longer defines me or who I am. It no longer controls my thoughts or my emotions. I am no longer in the "crying time." But without it, I would not be the person I am today. I would not be living this life. I would not have the people I have in my life, or the ones who were there in my past twenty years.

It may surprise a lot of you when I say, with a heart of truth, Thank You, Joe, for giving me the most amazing gift I will ever acquire in this lifetime. And you may say to yourself, Oh get real, Lady!!!

But it is true, and here is why:

#1-I lost my little house on Valleyway, and had to move into Valley Apartments, where I met my very special and dear friend Steven.

#2-I met Jack and Gayle and the pottery shop that I feel saved my life, and made the move to Copallis Beach, Washington.

#4-Moving to Aberdeen, where Steven brought Les into my life.

#5-Moving to Klamath Falls, Oregon, where we met Swami Ty.

Well, the list goes on and on. For without Joe, none of this would have happened. My life would have taken another path, and I am liking how this one is turning out, ha ha.

In Wayne W. Dyer's book, *Wisdom of the* Ages, (I would highly recommend any and all of his books, for they have helped me greatly) he quotes from Jalaluddin Rume, on grief, "I saw grief drinking a cup of sorrow and called out, 'it tastes sweet, does it not?' 'You've caught me,' grief answered, 'and you've have ruined my business, how can I sell sorrow when you know it's a blessing?'"

This has been a long and hard journey that I have been on. Have I acquired jewels in my crown? Who knows! Have I discovered silver linings along the way? Oh yes! That one I can answer. I have my sister Julia in my life! I have my best friend Les (aka Fez, Fezley, bro), in my life. I have wonderful stories to tell, wisdom to share, and a beautiful daughter, who has been there for me all the way.

I have a wonderful man, Swami Ty, who taught me how to meditate, how to retrieve my soul piece, and grow through forgiveness for myself and for Joe. Between him and Les they have shown me a path of enlightment to walk and to live an authentic and truthful life

Something else I have learned along this journey is that enlightment isn't something that you can own, something that you can acquire by being "good" or following the "right religion." It's something I cannot attain but before I know it, I have realized it. Everything changes, yet everything stays the same. I have changed. I feel and see things in a different light, with peace and with love. I am reprograming my brain. Oh please, remember this. I am not special. There are millions of stories we all have about our walk in the here and now, all of our silver linings, all the jewels in our crowns, all of our choices and decisions we have made. Some were more difficult than others, but look back, go ahead, look back. Look how far you have come!

While driving back from Sedona, and a wonderful retreat, I realized that I had come full circle, and what a huge circle it had become, a nineteen-year journey that I could now see, connected. I had to pull off the road because I did what I do best, yep! You got it, I cried buckets.

On to new and wonderful beginnings, new and fun adventures here in Payson, Arizona, with my bro. PEACE

AND LOVE AND LIGHT to all of you who have taken the time to read this very personal and heart-wrenching journey I have gone through. I desire, believe, and intend that it helps you find some answers, and the strength to live a truthful and loving life . . . .